Baptismal service in Silver Creek, Madison County
Kentucky ca early nineteen hundreds.

Beyond the Hills that Beckon

RAY LONG

EDITED BY
SHARON LONG

iUniverse, Inc.
Bloomington

Beyond the Hills that Beckon

iUniverse books may be ordered through booksellers or by contacting:

iUniverse
1663 Liberty Drive
Bloomington, IN 47403
www.iuniverse.com
1-800-Authors (1-800-288-4677)

ISBN: 978-1-4502-5982-8 (sc)
ISBN: 978-1-4502-5981-1 (ebook)

Printed in the United States of America

iUniverse rev. date: 12/08/2010

Contents

Ackowledgments   VII

Foreword   IX

Early Madison County   1

The Tudor's Entry   3

Meandering Memories Of Turner's Ridge   9

The Ross/Oliver Families   17

Doug Howard Reflections   31

The Shirley Land Family   38

Poosey Ridge Stories, A Little History And A Little Trivia   40

Poosey Potpourri   68

Recent Area Church Info   85

Area Clergymen   105

A Trip To The Holy Land   110

Poosey Ridge   118

Kirksville School   125

The Rural Demonstration School   135

Lancaster Pike   151

The Peytontown Baptist Church   164

Ramblings   170

Finale   180

ACKOWLEDGMENTS

The author wishes to thank the following individuals, without whose contributions this work would be lacking in content.

Gerald Tudor, for sharing the Tudor genealogy and valuable photographs.

Neal Burnam Whittaker, for his Poosey trivia and other important historical information.

The late Lucille Turner Whitaker Malear, whose granddaughter Dana Starnes provided interesting and factual information on Turner's Ridge and other areas.

Jacquelyn Ross Golden, for the invaluable information and dates on Kirksville school.

Betty Tevis King helped me piece together names and events at the Rural Demonstration School and Peytontown Baptist Church.

Earl "Doug" Howard: what can I say about Doug? He has been helpful in so many areas as the content of the book will reveal.

Glen Ross a distant relative who provided information on the Ross and Oliver families.

Alma Stone was kind enough to provide important documentation relative to the history and current events of the Corinth Christian Church.

Bobby Griggs whom I wish to thank for honoring me by adding the photo and nice article about "The Hills That Beckon" to his Poosey Ridge website.

Jesse Long grandson of the eldest son of my great grandfather Daniel Long,

Who is also Jesse's great grandfather has had insight on identifying certain family members of that branch.

Mary Laura Long Proctor (the author's aunt) was always available to answer questions concerning family history or incidents that happened in the Poosey area in the years past.

The late Edith Kanatzer Stocker a dear lady I have known most of my life, provided me with a photograph of the Friendship Church as well as some personal information regarding the old church.

A special thanks to our good friend Rhonda Bennett whose expertise in adding the photographs as well as other important additions is so appreciated.

FOREWORD

After the publication of the original "Hills That Beckon" in August of 2003, some might ask, why a sequel? I have been more than pleased in the manner in which the first book has been accepted, not only in Madison County but in areas far removed from the local points of interest. At the time of this writing, this is the fifth year since the initial publication, and during this period the question has been asked, "do you plan to write a sequel?" The answer was always an unequivocal no. However, as one year followed another I became aware of certain errors in the original text which needed to be corrected. It also became clear there was much more which could be written about the area and the people as well as many important landmarks which were not included in the first transcript. The word "Beyond" in the new title, alludes to the fact the author will not confine the writing to the area described in the previous work, but will go beyond the boundaries to include other areas. A distinct departure from the earlier work will include writings and material from other sources, such as inserting data from "my grandmother's scrapbook" as well as historic, factual and trivial contributions from others. Data and morsels of information will be inserted from "my grandmother's scrapbook" as related subject matter unfolds. Sadly, many who willingly contributed to the narrative of the "Hills That Beckon" were gone before it was published. Perhaps in some small way this new endeavor will be a tribute to their memory.

Since this writing is a continuation of "The Hills That Beckon", every precaution will be taken to insure repetition or duplication will be avoided and/or kept to a minimum. The text of this volume is in fact a departure from the original. Whereas, there was continuity of story line in "The Hills That Beckon," beginning in 1791 and ending in 1943, some might describe this narrative as a patchwork of narration, information, trivia and biographical sketches, some not related to the other. Still, the author feels this writing will fill in some important blanks "Hills" did not deal with.

EARLY MADISON COUNTY

The following data relating to the organization and development of present day Madison County was lifted from "Glimpses Of Historic Madison County Kentucky", competently authored by Jonathan T. and Maud Weaver Dorris.

At Hillsborough, North Carolina, on August 27,1774, Richard Henderson along with five others formed the Louisa Company. Their purpose was "to rent or purchase land" from the Indians west of the Allegheny Mountains. It appears that for more than a decade earlier the forerunner of this organization, Richard Henderson and Company had existed, and Daniel Boone had been active in its service in what is now Tennessee and Kentucky. The Louisa Company soon admitted several other North Carolinians to it's membership and changed its name to the Transylvania Company. On march 17, 1775, at Sycamore Shoals on the Watauga River, Richard Henderson and his associates purchased nearly 20,000,000 acres of land from the Cherokee Indians for merchandise worth about $50,000. Approximately two-thirds of the purchase was enclosed by the Kentucky, Ohio and Cumberland rivers. The remainder lay south of the Cumberland. The area thus acquired was named Transylvania and plans were hastened to settle it and obtain its recognition as a new English colony. Daniel Boone was engaged as early as March 10, 1775, to cut a trail and establish a settlement on the Kentucky River, a task which he soon accomplished. By the middle of June, 1775, a fort was completed in what is now Madison County, and the beginning of a town, which Virginia incorporated as Boonesborough, in October, 1779.

Virginia refused to recognize the existence of the Transylvania Colony and in December, 1776, created the county of Kentucky, which was later (1780) divided into Jefferson, Fayette and Lincoln counties. In 1784 Nelson was created and in 1785 Mercer and Madison counties were provided for.

A debt of gratitude is due Dr. and Mrs. Dorris for their superb achievement in documenting this much valued history of Madison County.

With the opening of what became known as the Wilderness Road and the construction of the Boonesborough fort, settlers began the westward expansion into that area of Kentucky from Virginia and the Carolinas. Those resilient pioneers who risked life and limb to create a new life for themselves and their families, needed a safe haven in which to determine the next step in their perilous expedition. At that time there were only two such locations available in Kentucky, Harrodsburg and Boonesborough. In February, 1777, Logan's Fort at St. Asaph (Stanford) was completed and occupied.

At the time of this western expansion, the Revolutionary War was beginning to heat up along the eastern seaboard which encouraged many hardy individuals who's desire for new lands and to see new horizons, to leave their homeland sooner than expected. Also, given that migration to the new world began in the early Seventeenth Century, 1600-1699, the eastern part of the country was becoming well populated, and like Daniel Boone, they wanted elbow room.

THE TUDOR'S ENTRY

The migration which began in the mid-seventeen seventies from Virginia and the Carolinas, brought many family names to Madison County which can still be found today. Among these is the Tudor family, of which I can trace my own family lineage to two such immigrates who came from North Carolina to the newly established Madison County around 1785 or shortly thereafter.

Before I continue, there is a Madison County resident which I owe a debt of gratitude. I will certainly thank personally as well as publicly, Gerald Tudor. I am amazed at the body of work, and can only guess the hours that went into his compiling of the Tudor genealogy. I feel greatly honored as well as humbled he was willing to share his blood, sweat and tears with me. I have had the pleasure of meeting Gerald only once, but we do communicate occasionally.

When I first occasioned to inspect Gerald's vast Tudor documentation, my first thought was, too many John Tudors. According to Gerald's research, It is uncertain exactly where John Tudor #I was born, however, it is believed he died in Surry County Virginia in 1721.

His son, John Jr., or John #II was born about 1720 probably in The Isle Of Wright County, Virginia, and died 1782 in Granville County North Carolina. His first marriage was to Elizabeth (?) about 1746-1747. They were the parents of Phoebe, Henry and John. His second marriage was to Elizabeth White, about 1762. Their issue was Valentine, Tabitha, Winifred, Blumer, Daniel and Anna or Ann. John #III was born in October of 1754 in Brunswick County Virginia and died in Madison County, Kentucky January 10, 1838. He served three tours of duty in the Revolutionary War and served in the North Carolina militia. He married Martha Searcy July 22, 1779 in Granville County North Carolina. They were the parents of twelve children, five of whom were born in North Carolina. They were Nancy, Oswald, Jane, Elizabeth and Patsy. Those born in Madison County were Samuel, Mary, John, Daniel, Henrietta, Morris and Marcus, also referred to as Mark.

As was mentioned, John Tudor began his migration to the much sought after land of Madison County Kentucky in 1785. There could have been quite a large assemblage, counting wife, children and siblings. His full sister, Phoebe was already married to John Morris who elected to remain in North Carolina. His full brother, Henry, moved to Madison County in 1787 and removed to Barren County Kentucky. John's half-siblings arrival in Madison County are listed in the following manner.

Valentine; Like John, served in the Revolutionary War. Was married in North Carolina and moved to Madison County in 1787.

Tabitha; married Pleasant Whitlow 1786 in North Carolina. They moved to Madison County in 1786. They must have remained in Madison for some time as Pleasant Whitlow sold two tracts of land to his brother-in-law, Samuel Moberly in the early 1800S', before moving on to Barren County Kentucky.

Blumer; It is possible that Blumer was among the followers who accompanied John and his company of adventurers to Kentucky. The record shows a Madison County marriage for Blumer in 1795.

Daniel; 1795 is also the year Blumer's brother, Daniel, married in Madison County.

Winefred,; Married John Long, December 1, 1791 in Madison County.

Anna; Married Samuel Moberly in Madison County, 1796.

4

It is written, "honest confession is good for the soul". There is an error, among many I am sure, to be found in the book "The Hills That Beckon." The book refers to the fact Winefred and Anna are sisters, which is true. It also states they are the daughters of John Tudor, which is also true, kind of. I can see how the reader would be led to believe the John Tudor who came to Madison County in 1785 was the father of Winny and Ann. Not true, their father was John Tudor #II or Jr., who died between January and May of 1782 in North Carolina. The John Tudor who came to Madison County was half-brother to the sisters. The fact that John signed the marriage bond for Winny and John Long could lead the readers to assume John III was the father, but not true.

My own family roots trace to the Tudor family through both Winefred and Anna or Ann. When Winefred married John Long in December of 1791, one of their sons, Daniel, sometimes referred to as Squire Daniel, married Anna Elizabeth Moberly, daughter of Samuel and Anna Tudor Moberly in January of 1834.

An interesting memory that I have about one of the above mentioned women: my grandfather, Leslie "Les" Long, who was born in 1890, discussed with me many years ago a memory of his grandmother, Anna Elizabeth Moberly Long, also known as Betty. He described how she would fatten a goose for a special occasion. He said she would prepare a coop with a wooden bottom. She would then put the goose inside the coop, tack the webbed feet to the floor of the coop so the goose could not move and then keep feed in front of the goose almost constantly. It would not take long for the goose to become plump and ready for the table. He said in that long ago era this was a common practice as how to fatten a goose.

According to certain Madison County records, John Tudor purchased various pieces of property before obtaining land on what became known as Poosey Ridge. Page #106 in the "Hills That Beckon," shows John Tudor became the owner of a tract of land purchased from Travis Million in 1818. This property is located across Poosey Ridge Road from the northwest corner of the present Gilead Baptist Church cemetery. There was a house on the property which became known as the John Tudor house. Did John build the house, or was it already there when he purchased the property? That question would be very difficult to answer at this point and time. Originally it was a two story log structure with an additional room added later. I think I can speak with some authority as to the structural design of the old house since I have stayed numerous nights and have enjoyed many meals there. When entering the front door, approximately half way across the front room there was a door to the right which led to a narrow spiral staircase to the upstairs. Proceeding through the front room, one was required to go down a couple of steps into what was used as the living room. The kitchen was the next room on this memory tour. As I recall, the rooms were rather large. The room which was added to the south side of the front room was a rather large room as well. The foundation of the new room was elevated which required steps to gain access to the door which faced east midway of the room. I mention this what to some may be a trivial matter, because I don't remember steps ever being there. As children, my cousins and me would make a game of jumping from, what we called the

high door, into the yard. My aunt, Mary Laura Long Proctor, who was born in April of 1917, advises she does not remember steps accessing the high door to the room. The terrain on which the house was built was unlevel, therefore, in order to level the floors, pillars to support the structure consisting of large flat limestone/sandstone rocks were fashioned to shore up the building. These hand crafted pillars, with stones of almost equal size stacked one upon the other reached heights from 2-½ to 3 feet. That's the way my memory recall registers it, such as it is at my age. At the back of the house where the pillars were located, my cousins and me found the area under the house an exciting place to play out of the sight of adult supervision. At some point in the long history of the old house, weatherboarding was added and painted white.

I have no knowledge as to the total acreage John Tudor purchased from Travis Million in 1818, but by the time my grandfather, Leslie "Les" Long, acquired the property in 1936, the land area had been reduced to 13-¾ acres.

In late 1943, Les Long sold the property to his brother, Samuel "Sam" Long who moved from his Moberly Branch location to his new purchase.

In the early to mid 1950's, Sam built a new home just north of the old house leaving it vacant and abandoned. After Sam died in July of 1982, the property was sold at auction and was purchased by neighbor, Duke Bellamy.

To summarize the life of John Tudor III in brief, he was born October 10, 1754 in Brunswick County, Virginia and died January 10, 1838 in Madison County, Kentucky. He served three tours of duty in the Revolutionary War, and was active in the North Carolina Militia. He married Martha Searcy in North Carolina in 1779. He and his family moved to the newly developed Madison County, Kentucky in 1785. Martha died sometime between 1810 and 1822. He then married Frances Phillips, a native of Garrard County. When John died in January of 1838, he was buried next to his first wife, Martha, in what became known as the Perry Long cemetery. This country cemetery is located in a field several yards across Poosey Ridge Road from the entrance to Dry Branch Road. November 5, 1975, at 3:00 P. M., there was a commemorative ceremony sponsored by the Boonesborough Chapter, Daughters of the American Revolution at the old cemetery honoring John's service. A marker was erected in his honor showing pertinent data.

It has been an honor for me to share, however briefly, some information relative to this pioneer family who was so influential in the life of early Madison County. Even though John III did not directly contribute to my personal genealogy, two of his half-sisters certainly did.

The John Tudor House

John Tudor Commemorative Marker

MEANDERING MEMORIES
OF TURNER'S RIDGE

Another family who were early residents of Madison County was the Cotton family. The Cottons settled the area which later became known as Turner's Ridge. The following term may, or may not be used as often as it once was, but I have heard people ask, "where is Cottonburg?" No doubt, that name was inspired by members of that family. To the casual observer, Cottonburg could be the name of a never-never land since no one seems to know exactly where it is. The old Cottonburg School was located at the intersection of present roads #876 and #595, which is in what is considered the upper part of Poosey Ridge. The store building which for years was known as Whitaker's store was built by Robert Long in 1904 for a son-in-law, Les Cotton. Another reason to identify Cottonburg with upper Poosey. However, Miss Emma Sowers store, which was located some distance north of the previous mentioned localities, served as a post office for the Cottonburg mail. Early in this segment, the author will reference his grandmother's scrapbook. In her scrapbook there are many obituaries clipped from the Richmond Daily Register which report the deaths of folk from what is considered upper to lower Poosey Ridge. Many of these whether upper or lower Poosey were given the address of Cottonburg. I'm sure, or at least I hope I will get many suggestions from readers where this mystic land of Cottonburg is to be found.

The following is a contribution from a descendant of the Cotton family which settled in Madison County early on.

Sometime after the publication of "The Hills That Beckon," I was honored by receiving a thirteen (13) page hand written letter from

Lucille Turner Whitaker Malear informing me how much she was enjoying the book and how she knew most of the people who were mentioned in the narrative, and a double honor for me, she added she had read the book several times. She also went on to say she could tell me much more which could be written about the area and the people. She also mailed subsequent letters from time to time.

Lucille was my third grade school teacher at Kirksville School, and had been a personal friend of my parents when my family lived in the area.

With Lucille's permission via a letter from her granddaughter, Dana Starnes, it is my pleasure and high honor to share with the readers a portion of some of the letters Lucille was kind enough to mail to me. Certain segments of her writings will be paraphrased while other sections will be direct quotes. When she mentioned the people, she said "I had a lot of them in school."

In chapter fifteen (15) in the "Hills That Beckon" there is a description of a contrivance referred to as a "dumb bull," the brainchild of Turner's Ridge resident, Bert Prather. This device in the hands of Bert was capable of producing unbelievable, mind-boggling sounds, especially at night. Lucille, whose family lived on the ridge, describes her first encounter with Bert's creation. In a direct quote from her letter she says, "you mentioned Bert Prather and the dumb bull, I know exactly how it sounded." She underlined several times the word, "exactly." She writes, "my sisters Ethel, Elma and I like to go visit our Grandmother. One dark night we took out lanterns and went to see Granny. As we were coming home we heard a funny sound. We started walking faster and the sound got louder and we thought it was some wild animal behind us. We started running and Ethel couldn't run fast, she was always heavy. We had a hard time pulling Ethel along and hold the lanterns. We almost fell in the door at home and was out of breath and could hardly talk to tell what happened." She went on to say her cousin, Vernon Coy, who lived in the same small house my family occupied from 1939 to 1941, was the co-conspirator along with Bert in terrorizing the young girls.

Vernon and Bert told Lucille's father, William Bourbon Turner, they had heard some kind of animal. They didn't know what it was, but it had an awful sound. She added her father had cleaned a plot of land to put in a crop of tobacco. She further explained back then they called it "new ground." This tract of land was in back of the Bert Prather residence. Bert and Vernon fashioned some type of pattern which would produce the likeness of an animal track when pushed into the dirt or mud. They made several imprints in the area where Bourbon was preparing to plow. Quoting Lucille again, "he went out to plow and heard this awful noise and saw the prints in the mud. He plowed a while and the noise grew louder. The old horse stuck up its ears and began to walk fast. Papa being afraid it was going to run, unhitched it and rode quickly to the house and told us about it."

Lucille continues with her account of the "dumb bull" when she says "I never knew what it was until I married Garnett Whitaker in 1932 and Bert told him all about it. He told me, but I never told the family because we all loved Bert and I didn't want them to know about it."

She departs somewhat from the actual occurrence when she shares "I was reading in "The Hills That Beckon" about the "dumb bull" when her husband, Harold said, "I have seen the one Bert made". She asked him to make one. He did not have the material that Bert used, but took a simple round oatmeal box, putting a small hole in the closed end of the box and attaching a button to the string so it would not pull through. He applied resin to the string and she said, "it worked." She continued by saying she and Harold lived in a retirement community and Harold could not go outside and pull the string for fear of un-nerving the old people.

From time to time, in her letter, Lucille refers to "the little house you lived in." Her father, William Bourbon Turner owned a rental house on the ridge where my family lived from 1939 to late 41 or early 42. Lucille writes, "my father built the little house for my mother's father in 1928. He died in 1929 and papa rented the house.

Lucille married Garnett Whitaker in 1932 and began their lives together in the little house her father built.

She relates a story regarding an incident when Garnett was plowing corn in a field between their residence and the Bert Prather home. Bert and his wife, the former Pearl Rhodus were the parents of two sons, Russell Dean, the eldest, and Cecil Francis. Garnett said he saw Russell coming toward the corn field. She said, "Russell was always full of mischief while Cecil was very quiet." Russell was standing at the edge of the corn field and each time Garnett would pass, Russell would throw small stones at the horse. This action would cause the horse to become disturbed causing some corn to be torn down. Each time Garnet passed, the same thing happened. Finally Garnett stopped and asked, "Russell, did you ever chew tobacco?" Russell replied he had never chewed, to which Garnett told him to bite off a chew and he would chew with him. He told him to chew it up real good and they would see who could spit the greatest distance. Russell was really having fun, but he finally spit out the tobacco and went to the house. In a few minutes he heard Pearl scream, "Garnett, come here and take Russell Dean to the doctor, Bert is not here, and Russell is dying." He tied his horse and ran to the house. Pearl said, "Russell is turning blue and is vomiting terrible." Garnett was forced to tell Pearl what he had done. In a few minutes Russell recovered completely.

Lucille reminded me in "The Hills Beckon" there was coverage given to the Reverend W. R. Royce, long time Madison County Baptist Minister. She shares the following story where the Reverend Royce was involved. She recounts she and Garnett had attended a Revival service at the Gilead Baptist Church where Royce was preaching. Reverend Royce, and I am only assuming, Mrs. Royce, Garnett and Lucille were invited to dinner at the home of Mr. and Mrs. Russell Ross. Mrs. Ross was the former Fannie Mae Calico. After a good meal, those in attendance were seated on the front porch. The Ross's son, Russell Jr., had a pet goat. It came from around the house and into the front yard. Royce said "Garnett, I'll bet you can't ride that goat." Garnett replied, "I'll bet I can." He walked up to the goat who was gentle and let him pet him. Garnett jumped on his back and grabbed him by his horns, and as Lucille describes it, "you have never seen a wilder ride." After several trips around the yard, the goat stopped suddenly causing the rider to pitch forward over the goat's head, landing in the grass. According to Lucille, "Royce laughed until the tears rolled down his cheeks." Royce turned to Lucille and said, "you should have a place waiting for you in heaven for living with that man."

I doubt Lucille was actually a member of Gilead at the time of the event described in the preceding paragraph. In one of her letters mailed in 2003, she disclosed she joined Gilead eighty four (84) years ago. She continued by saying all of her family went there. She was baptized at age nine in Joe Long's pond at Round Hill. After she and Garnett were married, she moved her membership to Salem Christian Church.

Lucille was kind enough to share some family history in another letter. Borrowing from Forrest Calico's book, "A Story of Four Churches", he states in the Gilead Baptist Church segment there were only two men active in the church during the Civil War. They were James Calico and William "Buck" Cotton. Buck Cotton was Lucille's great, great grandfather. Nathaniel Cotton was the eldest son of William and Elizabeth Prewitt Cotton. He had six surviving children; one of these was Sarah Belle Cotton, Lucille's grandmother. Sarah Belle married Cyrus Bonaparte Turner, who were the parents of the following children. William Bourbon Turner, Lucille's father. Miller Turner, died young. Squire Nathaniel Turner, Malinda Etta Turner, Susie Burton Turner, Ava or Ova Ellen Turner, Geneva Turner and Martha Turner.

Nathaniel Cotton, Lucille's great grandfather, owned 500 acres in the Turner Ridge area as well as some property in Garrard County. The land was divided among the heirs with Sarah Belle Cotton Turner obtaining several acres of land.

The Nathaniel Cotton home was located on the portion of the ridge which runs north and south past Bourbon's rental house and back in the field toward Dry Branch. Lucille's sister, Ethel, describes the home as being built of log, with weather boarding and black shutters. Ethel goes on to say it was a pretty home. Evidently the Turner family lived there for a while. Lucille says she was born in this house in 1911 and her sisters Ethel and Elma would walk down the hill to Dry Branch and up the hills to the Hendren School on Poosey Ridge road. Several years ago Lucille mailed me a sketch of this house superbly implemented by her sister Ethel. I personally do not remember this home as it burned many years before I became a resident of Turner's Ridge.

An observation: In 1877, Allen Taylor and his wife, Josephine, deeded one (1) acre of land to the trustees of the Gilead United Baptist Church. The trustees were Nathaniel Cotton, Lucille's Great Grandfather, and Jacob Moberly, brother of my Great, Great Grandmother, Elizabeth Moberly Long. This deed says nothing about being on Poosey Ridge Road, but is described as being on Goggins Ferry Road. The transaction was entered by the court May 10, 1877.

William Bourbon Turner, his wife, the former Mary Hughes, and family resided in this home until Lucille was three (3) years old. The family then moved to another house on the ridge. During the period my family lived there, it was the home of, among others, the Irvin Davis family.

Lucille's grand-mother lived in the house, according to Lucille, where the Malear family lived. I clearly recall the Malear's living there. This home was still in use as a dwelling the last time I visited that area.

The Cotton family was still very much in evidence when my family were Turner Ridge residents. At the end of the ridge road beyond the Bert Prather residence was the home of Mrs. Mollie Ross and her family. This property was owned by Brutus Cotton, a descendant of the Cotton families who settled this area.

As of this writing, Lucille is in her ninety seventh (97) year and is still very clear of mind. She will never fully know how I appreciate her sharing with me many of her remembrances.

After almost fifty (50) years of marriage, Lucille lost her husband, Garnett, July 15, 1981. He was described in his obituary as being a native of Madison County, a retired farmer and a member of the Salem Christian Church.

Lucille's second marriage was to Harold Malear. Harold was the son of Alfred and Mary Sowers Malear. As a young man, Harold had lived in the same house as Lucille's grand-mother, Sarah Belle Cotton Turner. My family and the Malears were neighbors for a period of time. He had lost his wife, the former Jamie Whitaker. I had been privileged to be able to renew my relationship with Lucille and Harold at the Gilead Baptist Church home comings. I saw them last at the home coming event in September, 2006. I was shocked and saddened when I learned of Harold's death July 19, 2007.

I knew Lucille's father, William Bourbon Turner, her aunt, Malinda Etta Turner, who we referred to as Miss Etta as well as her sister, Ethel. Ethel was a teacher at Kirksville where I saw her on an almost daily basis as well as the Gilead Baptist Church each Sunday. However, I was not acquainted with her sister Elma. Elma Belle Turner Cox(Robert) was born November 11, 1904 and died January 30, 2000.

Ethel Turner Cates, as mentioned was a school teacher for many years at Kirksville, as was her sister, Elma. She was a long time member of the Gilead Baptist Church and served as church clerk. Ethel preceded her two sisters, Lucille and Elma in death. She was also survived by her husband, John Cates.

Author's note: As this narrative was in the process of being scripted, I received the sad news of the death of Lucille Turner Whitaker Malear, March 10, 2009 age 97.

Poosey Ridge boys at the property of the former Sarah Belle
Cotton Turner on Turner's Ridge. L-R Shelby Joe Masters,
Buddy Goodlet, Herndon R. Agee, James M. Campbell,
Doug Howard, Leslie "Shorty" Davis and Curtis C. Davis.

THE ROSS/OLIVER FAMILIES

In the book, "The Hills That Beckon", the Long family was used as a conduit to tell a story which included many other people. In like manner, this author will draw on two particular people whose memory has not faded with the passage of time. An attempt will be made to weave together two Poosey Ridge families, the Ross family of Turner's Ridge and the Oliver family of Hendren's Ridge. Both families received limited coverage in the above mentioned book, however, like so many other families in the area, there is much more which can be said.

A brief genealogy of the Ross and Oliver family will follow with some comments inserted, sometimes for clarification and/or story value. In "The Hills That Beckon" It was believed Mrs. Mollie Ross was the granddaughter of Albert Marion Long, my great grandfather's brother. However, this has been proven to be untrue. She was the daughter of John S. Long, possibly a distant relative.

As was related in "The Hills That Beckon" I was very familiar with Mrs. Mollie Ross and many of her children, having visited in that home on numerous occasions. However, to my memory I had never met nor seen Mr. Tommie Ross as he had died in 1938 when I was four years old.

Hiram Thomas "Tommie" and Mollie Long Ross and their children

Hiram Thomas Ross: B 1879, D 1938
Mollie Long: B 1884, D 1963

Children

Macey Ross: B 1903, D 1910
Nellie Ross: B 1905, D 1992
Elizabeth Ross: B 1907, D 1982
John T. Ross: B 1909, D 1970
Anna Lee Ross: B 1913, D 1997
Charles Ross: B 1915, D 1996
Ira Preston Ross: B 1918, D 1980
Cecil Ray Ross: B 1920, D 1988
Andrew J. Ross: B 1923, D 1971
Ella Mildred Ross: B 1927, D 1982

Children of Tommie and Mollie Ross
Front Row L-R Nellie, Mildred
Back Row L-R Ira, Cecil, Charles, Ann and Liz
John T and Andrew J. deceased

Mollie Ross, about 1961

Before the Ross/Oliver narrative continues further, there is a descendant of these two families who deserves my gratitude and deep respect. A true native of the Poosey Ridge area, and one who is dedicated to preserving his family heritage for the benefit of his descendants, as well as needy historians like me. Glendon A. Ross is the son of Ira and Viola Oliver Ross, and now a resident of Garrard County. Glen has gone into great detail in establishing genealogical data on both family lines. It was through his research the accurate information on the father of his grandmother, Mollie Long Ross was disclosed. His generosity in sharing the genealogy of the two families as well as family photos are very much appreciated.

I cannot say with any accuracy that I actually remember all of the surviving Ross children, however, many I recall clearly.

Ella Mildred, whom family and friends referred to as Mildred was closer to my age. One clear memory I have of Mildred is, as the rest of the local school children walked the distance from where they lived on Turner's Ridge, Mildred rode her bike along with us. I did not think anything of it at the time, but when we got to the intersection of Turner's Ridge and Poosey Ridge Road, to ride the big yellow bus to Kirksville School, she would lean her bicycle against the fence and leave it for the day. She assumed it would be there when she returned in the afternoon, and it always was. Everyone knew it was Mildred Ross's bike, and no one ever considered taking it or even riding it without her permission. I doubt that anyone on Turner's Ridge, or Poosey Ridge, for that matter ever locked their doors when leaving home. What an amazing, and disappointing difference in the culture of the early nineteen forties compared to today.

I remember Nellie Ross Isaac clearly as well as her husband Charles who was commonly known as "Charlie." Nellie was a bit older than my parents she being born in 1905 and my parents in 1912. The Isaac's attended The Gilead Baptist Church in the early nineteen forties as did my family. Nellie and Charlie were the parents of two daughters, Doraleen and Judith or Judy. Doraleen was two or three years older than me and I remember her distinctly. However, the memory is not clear of Judy, Perhaps it is due to the fact she was still an infant when we departed that area in late nineteen forty three.

When I think of the Ross children my mind seems to focus more on Ira than the others. He was only six years younger than my Dad, therefore, it was common for Ira to stop by the house for a visit. Also, our barn was near a section of the ridge road which led to the Ross home, and when my Dad was working at the barn, it was convenient for Ira to stop by and pass the time of day.

I knew Andrew "A. J." and Cecil, but not as well as the preceding three. The Poosey Ridge area was awash with practical jokers who were not reluctant to display their humor on whomever was available. A. J. and Cecil had some hunting dogs they were very proud of. The two Ross boys had stopped at Creighton Whittaker's store to loaf with some of the perpetual loafers. Being aware of their fondness for their dogs, someone made the announcement to the group, the Madison County dog catcher was in the area and any dog not having a dog tag would be confiscated and the owner fined. The Ross boys excused themselves and raced toward home. The story goes it was a sight to behold to see Cecil and A. J. running down the hill in back of their home toward Paint Lick Creek with a dog under each arm.

I'm not sure where the preceding story originated, but someone told my father who in turn told it to me.

After our family moved to Lancaster Pike, A. J. stopped by to visit on at least one occasion. It was always good to see someone from Poosey Ridge.

Glen Ross, who seems to have emerged the chronicler and biographer of his family, was kind enough to share the following short story which no doubt, has remained in the Ross family many years. This is an account which, in all probability, will continue to survive in this family as the years unfold. Glen was born several years after the death of his grandfather, but family legend has preserved the saga in detail. The following will be presented as it was communicated to me, in print.

The Rabbit that shot Pap Tommie

Tommie was rabbit hunting on Poosey Ridge around 1928. He jumped a rabbit and it ran into a large brush pile. Determined to get the hare, Tommie leaned the gun against the brush pile as he began to move limbs and branches to scare the rabbit out of its hiding place. His efforts were rewarded and the rabbit scampered for freedom. In a strange twist of fate, the rabbit bumped the shotgun, it fell, and discharged. The shot struck Tommie in the foot. The complications from this accident, infection eventually required amputation of his lower leg. Tommie suffered great pain from this accident and became addicted to pain killers (probably morphine). After enduring this situation for several years, Granny Ross displayed her determination by helping him withdraw "cold turkey" from the medication. His last years were spent with pain but free of the medication.

Ira and Viola Oliver Ross and son, Glendon A
(Glennie) fishing in Paint Lick Creek

Glennie and Donnie Ross Children of Ira and Viola

At this point in the narrative, the weaving together of the Ross and Oliver families begins its progression and will reveal how my own family is connected to these two families.

Robert Oliver, whom I knew well, will be referred to as the patriarch of this particular branch of the Olivers. He was born in Virginia in 1889 and migrated with his family to Kentucky around 1900. His first marriage was to Maggie Lowe in 1907. They were the parents of two sons, Luther and Leamon, born in Knox County. Maggie died rather young, and after this sad event Robert and the two boys moved to Madison County around 1918.

It did not take Robert long to get re-settled into domestic living after coming to Madison County. I have a copy of a Marriage Certificate(supplied by Glen Ross)showing a marriage between Robert Oliver, age 29 and Jennie Long, age 15, September 10, 1918. The witnesses were Dan Long, father of the bride, and my great grandfather and Mrs. Annie Long, my grandmother and sister-in-law to the bride. The certificate was signed by W. K. Price, county judge.

Now, my branch of the Long family is connected to the Oliver family. Jennie is the sister of my grandfather, Les Long, hence, Jennie is my great aunt.

The following is a listing of Robert and Jennie M. Long Oliver and their children.

Robert Berry Oliver B. 1889 D. 1956
Jennie M. Long B.1904 D. 1983

Children

Zora A. Oliver B. 1920
Lonzie E. Oliver B. 1921 D. 2005
James Marvin Oliver B. 1924 D. 1991
Viola Estill Oliver B. 1926 D. 1968
Elwood Robert Oliver B. 1929 D. 2006
Edna Marie Oliver B. 1931

The Robert Oliver family at a gathering on the day his son, Lonzie, was leaving to serve in WWII, July 1942. Luther and Jewell are at the right end with their two sons, L.B. and Leon. Immediately to the left of Robert and Jennie are Leamon and Hallie and their oldest son, Paul Burnham. Elwood and Edna are at the left of the picture. Lonzie, and his bride to be, Anna Mildred Hume, are directly behind Edna. Zora and Della are behind their oldest son Norman, (the smallest boy in front) Marvin is hidden behind Jennie. Ira and Viola were not able to attend.

Robert Oliver had the reputation of being a kind, generous and helpful individual. He was a farmer and a very skilled carpenter. He was a religious man and very instrumental in the building of The Poosey Methodist Church. When he died in 1956, my grandmother, Annie Long wrote a letter giving us the sad news of his death. She also commented, at the viewing she encountered person after person who could not say enough about what a good and kind man he was. I remember him well and at this point in my life count it an honor to have known him.

Robert Oliver and his six sons. L-R in chronological
order: Luther, Leamon, Zora, Lonzie, Marvin and
Elwood. Their father Robert is in the middle in back.

I remember as well who my father referred to as Aunt Jennie. I
remember her as a soft spoken, unassuming woman. I saw her last
at her brother's funeral, when Samuel Long died in the summer of
1982.

Most of the Oliver children were older than me, and as a result
there was little camaraderie except for Elwood and Edna. I soon
found Elwood, like me, was a western movie fan whose favorite
movie cowboy was Hopalong Cassidy.

It seems cupid was active in the Poosey area in the early nineteen
forties, as a romance began to blossom between Ira Ross and Viola
Oliver. It is not clear how this courtship was ignited, or where. At
this point and time there were many farewell parties given for local
fellows going into WWII. The following is an example of such an
event as it appeared in the Richmond Daily Register in the very early
nineteen forties. Again, courtesy of my grandmother's scrapbook, of
which there was no date, other than the month and day of the week.

WIENER ROAST

Miss Roberta Long entertained with a wiener roast Thursday night August 5th, in honor of Mr. George Goodlett Jr., and Mr. Darnell Taylor who recently enlisted in the U. S. Marine Corps. Those present were Misses* Dorothy Goodlett, Mildred McCoy, Anna Mae Prather, Clarice Whitaker, Wilma Peyton , Margaret Hamm, Jewel Dean Long and Clyde Long. Messrs* Franklin Whitaker, Russell Dean Prather, Dowell Layton, Frank Taylor, Nelson Whitaker, Lonnie Elswick, Marvin Oliver, Clifford Anglin, Bufford Singer, Sterling Moberly, Harold Dean Rogers and Elwood Oliver.

It is possible one of these could have been the setting for this amorous adventure. Roberta Long, who is my aunt, was married in 1942. Since she was referred as Miss in the article helps to determine the approximate date of the gathering. Notice, Viola's brothers, Marvin and Elwood were present.

* At this time it was common to refer to a collection of young ladies as Misses and young fellows as Messrs.

Other family members perceive it is possible the occasion of this memorable meeting could have taken place at an event at the Gilead Baptist Church or Salem Christian Church. Regardless of where or how the introductions were made, Ira Preston Ross and Viola Estill Oliver were married January 10, 1942 in Richmond Kentucky.

With four of her five sons' in the military, Ira, being married chose to remain at home and see to the welfare of his widowed mother and manage the farm.

It was during the period, 1939 through 1943 I became well acquainted with Mrs. Mollie Ross, Ira, Andrew "A. J.", Cecil and Mildred. Our family had moved to Dry Branch in late 1942, just down the hill from Turner's Ridge. It was a short walk up the hill to where my grandfather and grandmother Anglin lived. In fact, it was the same house Ira and Viola moved to after the other Ross boys returned from military service. This was also the same house where the William Bourbon Turner family lived.

My uncle, Clifford Anglin who was around seventeen years old at the time, was still living at home and was also very well acquainted with the Ross family. Somewhere, Clifford had picked up a type of disguise device, probably in Richmond. It was a simple contrivance, with ear pieces similar to reading glasses and made of plastic with large bulging eyes, a bulbous nose and a rather heavy black mustache. When put on, the wearer resembled the old comedian, Jerry Colonna. This particular evening I happened to be visiting my grandparents when Clifford suggested the two of us visit the Ross household. It was already dark when we arrived and Clifford asked me to go on in while he would be in later. There was a light and some activity in the kitchen and as was my custom, I strode boldly in. Viola was seated in a kitchen chair with a wash pan and was proceeding to wash her feet. After a few minutes of polite conversation, Clifford walked through the kitchen door wearing the disguise. When Viola saw the strange intruder, she let out a piercing scream. When Clifford saw she was disturbed, he immediately but laughingly removed the contrivance. When she saw who the culprit really was, she said, "Rinkie Anglin, I'm going to knock you in the head for scaring me that way." Clifford had lived in that community for many years and, as a child, had acquired the nickname of "Rinkie." I called him by that name, or "Rink" until I became aware it was an embarrassment to him. I programmed myself to call him simply, Cliff.

Clifford Anglin, as he looked when he frightened Viola

In the segment, "Meandering Memories Of Turner's Ridge" Lucille Malear stated her family moved into a house on Turner's Ridge when she was three years old. This would have been around 1914. When Ira's brothers returned from serving in WWII, and take over the management of the 140 acre family farm, this is the same house where Ira and Viola moved.

Borrowing a few lines from a paragraph in a document mailed to me by Ira and Viola's son Glen, he writes, "Dad would try to support his family by farming on Poosey. However, like nearly all the boys who came back to Poosey from the war, Dad would soon realize that the small family farm would not support his family. Thus begins an odyssey in which all the Ross children would move to urban areas and leave the the farm behind." Glen goes on to describe the avenue each aunt and uncle took when they left the farm, and Ira, his father, became a trucker.

Ira and Viola were the parents of two sons, Glendon Allen "Glennie" Ross, born August 11, 1946, an Donald "Donnie", born November 3, 1950.

I must admit I sat before the screen of my word processor for an undetermined amount of time, hesitant I could not find the right words to verbalize the following portion of this narrative. I have determined there are no right words to describe this sad event. I apologize for the matter of fact method in which this tragedy is presented. Thanks once again to Glen Ross for the details involving the horrific accident which took the life of his mother, Viola Estill Oliver Ross in July of 1968.

Viola, her son Donnie, who was driving, her mother Jennie and her sister Edna, who were in the back seat, were en route to the Smoky Mountains for some vacation time. They were driving south on U. S. 25 in Laurel County north of London, Kentucky when the accident occurred. The pavement was wet from a recent thunderstorm, and a 1967 Camaro occupied by two young men apparently over corrected, sped across the center line in the path of the Ross's oncoming vehicle. Everyone in the Ross car was injured seriously. Jennie's leg was broken in several places. Edna was also seriously injured. Viola died in the ambulance before arriving at Good Samaritan Hospital in Lexington. The two young men in the Camaro were killed instantly. I can recall how upset our family was when we received the sad report about Viola. Glen's brother, Donnie had no memory of the accident. It was Glen's painful duty to tell his brother about the death of their mother as he lay recovering in the hospital.

There were member's of the Ross family who migrated to Lawrenceburg. Kentucky as the years continued to unfold. As one by one, they departed the old farm on Turner's Ridge to create and develop career's of their own, it was clear their mother, Mollie would not be able to remain there alone. They actually had no thought of leaving her there. She died in 1963 at the home her children had provided for her in Lawrenceburg. They also were considerate enough to provide a caregiver when she became too ill to care for herself.

Jennie Long Oliver moved from the farm on Hendren's Ridge in 1958 where she and Robert had raised their children, she moved in with her daughter, Edna and husband, Bennie until her death in 1983.

It was mentioned at the beginning of this segment, these two families were given limited attention in "The Hills That Beckon." It has been my honor to render a more in depth characterization of these two families.

Again, I wish to extend credit and appreciation to Glen Ross, son of Ira and Viola Oliver Ross for providing statistical data and photographs as well as other essential information.

Author's note: In my own personal opinion it is unlikely Ira and Viola met at one of the going away parties for fellows going into the Armed Services since they were married January 10, 1942. War had only been declared about a month at this time and I doubt many in this area had been called or even volunteered at the time.

Doug Howard Reflections

When the book, "The Hills That Beckon" was published around the first of September, 2003, I was surprised, and pleased to receive a phone call from Earl Douglas "Doug" Howard. He was very complimentary and said the story was very much like his own while growing up in the Poosey Ridge area. Since that time I have been privileged to communicate and spend some quality time with Doug. It is amazing, and perhaps not coincidental that after all these years we were able to renew our relationship. Doug, his brother Gene and me were playmates as small children, but the fact I moved to another state, there was no contact with either for many years.

Doug is very proud of the fact he is the seventh generation of the Howard family living in Kentucky since the arrival of James Howard in 1791, a year prior to Kentucky statehood.

The following is not intended to be a genealogical search of the Howard family. In fact it will begin with a paraphrase of an obituary of Doug's maternal grandfather, Henly Whitaker. Some may ask, why list the pallbearers and the honorary pallbearers? All the men listed were respected and familiar names in this area of Madison County and many folk today remember, if not the men themselves, the names.

This obituary appeared in the Richmond Daily Register in 1942. The article is another selection from my grandmother's scrapbook. The article itself was not dated, nor did my grandmother date it. It will be paraphrased and not a direct quote.

Henly Whitaker, 61, Cottonburg farmer, died at the Gibson Hospital at 12:20 this morning after an illness of four years.

He is survived by four daughters. Mrs. Lawrence(Bernice) Campbell, Mrs. Rexford(Emma Lee)Reynolds, Mrs. Garnett(Dorothy Faye) Howard and Mrs. Harold(Jamie) Malear, all of Madison Co. Two sisters, Mrs. John Baily, Iowa and Mrs. Lizzie Whitaker, Richmond. Two brothers, Dock Whitaker, Lexington and Thomas Whitaker, Richmond. Mr. Whitaker was a member of The Gilead Baptist Church. Funeral arrangements have not been completed pending the arrival on a son-in-law, Harold Malear, now in the army. Burial will be held in the Richmond Cemetery with the Reverend A. E. Gibson of Georgetown, officiating.

Active pallbearers will be; Henderson Whitaker, Garnett Whitaker, James Russell Whitaker, Lewis Whitaker, Hisle Whitaker and Robert Price Whitaker.

Honorary pallbearers; Creighton Whitaker, E. C. Tussey, Charlie Isaacs, Wolford Agee, Nathan Moore and Earl Hendren.*

*Doug feels it was Earl and not Carl, as printed in the obit.

Nothing was said in the obituary about Mrs. Henley Whitaker as she had preceded him in death by several years. Her name was Sally Whitaker, possibly a third cousin, which was quite common at the time.

One of Henly's four surviving daughters was Dorothy Faye Whitaker Howard. Dorothy's husband, Garnett Howard, was the son of Fred Napoleon Howard and Jessie Moberly.

Garnett and Dorothy were the parents of two sons, Gene Bernard, born December 3, 1932 and Earl Douglas, born June 15, 1935.

Like most farm families, Garnett and Dorothy moved from place to place for a period of time before settling down to their own property on Poosey Ridge Road.

Doug first saw the light of day on the farm of Elbert Murphy where his father was renting that year. This farm was near Round Hill. Doug shared a few details about this memorable event. I'm sure it was memorable to his mother, and not to Doug. He says the day before his birth, his mother dropped tobacco plants all day from a coal bucket. His father, Garnett, borrowed Elbert Murphy's car to summon the doctor. This is a direct quote from Doug, "Elbert Murphy's wife, Geneva, put the first rag of clothes on me I ever wore."

Gene and Doug grew up at the property purchased from Hugh or Hughey Rhodus on Poosey Ridge road near Miss Emma Sower's store. Early on Gene acquired the name "Tarp." According to Doug, while Gene was attending Poosey School, he was surprised and actually frightened by the sudden appearance of a Terrapin. Since this land reptile was pronounced "Tarpin" by most folk in the area(me included)he began to be known by his peers as "Tarp." Doug said few people who were acquainted with Gene actually knew his real name.

To describe this next episode in the Howard family, I will attempt to be as sensitive and discreet as possible. Many folk who read this account will not understand, especially those in urban areas. In a farming community such as Poosey, it was quite common for certain farmers to maintain bulls as part of their herd. It was also common for people who had milk cows and required the service of a bull when their cows went dry, to take their cow to a local farmer who kept a bull. There was usually no charge for this service, but an accommodation by one neighbor to another.

To help reinforce my poor explanation, I will refer once again to my good friend, Neal B. Whittaker who offers the following little gem.

Neal's father, C. W. Whitaker, was an enterprising man with varying interests, cattle being one of them. On an occasion when Mr. Whitaker was away from the store, a fellow named Virgil Alcorn came in and asked to see Mr. Whitaker. Mrs. Whitaker, Mable, asked if she could help him. Mr. Alcorn, who was reluctant to share the reason of his mission with a woman, finally said "I was wondering if Mr. Whitaker might have a gentleman cow I could borrow?"

Even though the prelude to this next adventure by one of the Howard boys was no doubt too lengthy, it sets the scene.

Gene's father, Garnett, asked him to take one of their cows to a local farmer's "gentleman cow." Doug said on the way back home, Gene was actually riding the cow, who from time to time would get into a trot. Doug also said the neighbor's were laughing and waving to him as he passed.

Life for a farm boy can be filled with satisfying adventure as well as irritation from time to time. Doug shared one such example of good intentions gone awry. Earlier in the day his mother had noticed an egg in the hen house. She asked Doug to get it as there was only one and she needed it as she was preparing supper. Obedient son that he was, Doug went immediately to retrieve the egg. With egg in hand he began the trek to the house when his father called to him and asked him to bring in the cows as it was milking time. He turned, still with egg in hand and proceeded to drive in the cows. When the cows were driven to the location where they were normally milked, there were either gnats, bees or cow flies which swarmed and excited the cows causing them to run back to whence they had come. This action angered and frustrated Doug to the point he actually threw the only egg on the place at one of the cows. The heartbreak of it all, he missed the cow. When the cows were back to their milking station, Doug volunteered to help milk or do any other chore which was in need of attention. The attempts of avoiding his mother failed and he was forced at last to face the music. He did not share in detail the depths of his mothers displeasure, but it was clear it was not pleasant.

The two Howard boys, Gene, "Tarp" and Doug spent the majority of their elementary and high school educational experience at Kirksville, As referenced earlier in the account of "Tarp" and the Terrapin, this event happened at the Poosey School which he attended only two years. Doug's entire school tenure was at Kirksville.

The following subject matter concerning the Howard brothers was shared personally with me by Doug. I trust I will be able to express the sensitivity and depth of feeling the story deserves. As is the case with some family members, when attaining adulthood, many seem to go their separate ways. Both Gene and Doug followed their own pursuits, not keeping in contact with each other as much as they possibly should have. According to Doug, the brothers saw less and less of each other as time progressed. One evening in August of 1984 Doug was driving on the bypass in Richmond and was stopped at a red light at the intersection of Lancaster Avenue. In the vehicle next to him he recognized his brother, "Tarp," whom he had not seen in a while. They each lowered their windows and were able to spend ten to fifteen seconds in conversation before the light turned green and they went their respective way. Doug was contacted approximately one half hour later to find his brother, "Tarp" had lost his life in an auto accident.

Doug also shared he could not help but believe there was an unseen hand guiding the two brothers to a final encounter for this brief moment in time.

In many families there are heirlooms which are dear to the hearts of certain family members. Some of these cherished mementos have survived literal decades of symbolic honor and respect. This is no less true among the members of the Howard family. The following is the story of such an artifact. The American College Dictionary defines the word "artifact" as follows. "Any object made by man with a view to subsequent use." The actual history of this artifact is obscure, as to who fashioned it or who was the first owner. Even though its beginning may be shrouded in mystery, the object itself is still very much with us. Without further embellishment or verbal expansion, the saga of "The Little Red Chair" will be passed along as it was conveyed to the author. The little chair was not always red, but received a generous application of red paint later on in its varied history. From what has been shared concerning the item in question, it certainly did enjoy subsequent use as the term artifact was defined.

Garnett Howard, Doug's father was born in 1909. When he was a small child he, along with his parents would visit his grandparents from time to time. Garnett's grandfather was Will Tom Moberly, son of Squire Moberly. At this point in our genealogies, Doug and the author can claim a little kin. Squire Moberly and the author's great great grandmother, Elizabeth Moberly Long were brother and sister. Doug is no doubt relieved the relationship is not close enough to do any damage. During one of the visits, Doug's father became enchanted with a little chair. He would sit in the chair, carry it or push it along the floor. He was so enraptured, when it was time for his family to leave, he quietly placed the new found treasure in the wagon or buggy or whatever the means of transportation. When Garnett's father, Fred, discovered his attempt to smuggle the prized possession away from the rightful owners, he was instructed to return the chair and make amends for his misdeeds. When his grandfather saw how enamored he was with this supposedly insignificant piece of furniture, he decided to make him a gift of it. The term "insignificant" was used in describing the little chair, but it certainly was not insignificant to Garnett nor to future generations of the Howard family which will become clear as this account unfolds.

When the little chair became a permanent fixture in the home of Garnett's father Fred, it was destined to be the object of delight for future generations of the Howard family. Even though, no doubt, Garnett considered the new found object of admiration his very own, I'm sure he had to share it with some, or all of six brothers from time to time. There was Kirby, Clyde, Carter, Delbert, Buford and Orville who had to take their turn.

Prior to the death of Jessie Moberly "Granny" Howard, in 1968, she gave this prized heirloom to her son Garnett. Up to this time, the little chair had retained it's natural wood finish. It was not until it became the property of the Garnett Howard family that Dorothy, Doug's mother, painted the little chair red. From this time forward, this tiny piece of furniture has been referred to as "The Little Red Chair."

After Garnett's death, Doug's mother Dorothy, gave the chair to him, and his kids played with it through their growing up experience.

Doug then passed the chair on to his son Michael, who was so impressed with the gift he was inspired to write a poem honoring this small artifact which had remained intact through several Moberly and Howard generations.

The following is Doug's son Michael's poem

The Little Red Chair

It's not fancy, it's not frilly
It's just a little red chair, seems so silly

It was here, way before me
Likewise long after, it shall be

It never broke, it never fell
How many it's sat, I couldn't tell

Daddy, down to me
We all used it, as happy as can be

From time to time, it might of got dusty,
But never never did it get rusty

Yes that little chair has amused many
Try to find a better chair? There isn't any

A new generation has taken over the little chair
And when they want, it it will be there

There were better gadgets or a toy
But it's awful special to this old boy

Michael Douglas Howard 03/1991

We will hear from Doug again in the Kirksville School segment.

THE SHIRLEY LAND FAMILY

Another family who has deep roots in the Poosey area is the Land family.

Shirley and Iva, or Ivie(Ivy), the patriarch and matriarch of this family were the parents of ten (10) children.

The author was privileged to know personally only a few of the ten descendants of Mr. and Mrs. Shirley Land.

Some of my earliest memories include Wilburn "Bib" Land as we rode the school bus to Kirksville school. I was in the first grade, while he could have very well been a senior in high school. He seemed to get a kick out of kidding me, in a good natured way, of course.

I recall Burdette very well. He was a successful contractor in the area. It was Burdette's company who built the new Salem Christian Church in th early nineteen fifties. The author's father was one of Burdette's employees in late nineteen forty nine and early nineteen fifty.

I had seen Clyde from time to time when I was a youngster at one of the Gilead revivals or at Whitaker's store. However, in the nineteen eighties, when The Gilead Baptist Church began to have their annual home comings, and Clyde and his wife, Eleanor became regular attenders, it was my distinct pleasure to be able to renew my relationship with Clyde. I looked forward from year to year to having a conversation with him. He seemed to enjoy our time together as I certainly did.

Based on the information I have been given, I understand the Land family lived on The New Road for quite some time before moving south on Poosey Ride Road.

To the best of the author's ability, a list of the names of the ten Land children will be presented.

They are as follows, not in chronological order.

Herbert

Burdette

Virgil "Jack"

Clyde

Wilburn "Bib"

Gilbert

Russell

* Elmer

Amy

Elsie

* Died in WWII

POOSEY RIDGE STORIES, A LITTLE HISTORY AND A LITTLE TRIVIA

WHITAKER'S STORE

In the book, "The Hills That Beckon" the name, Neal Burnam Whittaker is found several times. It would be difficult to write in depth about Poosey and not mention Neal B. When "Hills" was being written, I used him often for reference and questions concerning the area. While he still lived in Madison County, I referred to him as the resident Poosey Ridge authority. He now resides in Johnson City, Tennessee.

Several years ago I was surprised to receive by mail a rather lengthy list of Poosey Ridge trivia. The cover sheet said not for publication, but when I read it I contacted Neal to ask if I could use it if ever I wrote a sequel to "The Hills That Beckon," since I saw nothing offensive in its content. Neal answered promptly and did in fact give his permission to use his trivia questions and answers. I received his letter of permission December 4, 2005. When Neal B. learned I was serious about writing a sequel, he mailed me two additional hand written copies of reminiscences, one focusing on life around Whitaker's store, and the other an account of other country stores in the area. Neal B., an honest to goodness Kentucky Colonel, was born July 25, 1920 to Creighton and Mable Teater Whitaker. Some years ago Neal decided to add an extra "T" to his last name which accounts for the difference in the spelling of his name and his fathers.

The following contribution is in Neal's own words with only slight alterations for clarity and readability.

Madison County Kentucky is a big county. Lots of people travel many miles to work or to go shopping. One day we find ourselves at the Courthouse yard in Richmond. We see knife trading, talkers of politics, and then someone will ask, where is Poosey Ridge? Then someone will say. "O. K., you go to Lancaster Avenue, take a left to the Barnes Mill Road to Silver Creek and go across the bridge. Go up Page Hill, then in about one mile you will arrive at a large country store. You will notice the sign that reads, C. W. Whitaker, General Merchandise.

Inside this store you will see a big stock of goods. Groceries on the shelves, hardware, clothing, fruit etc.

Here I think you will find real human, motherly wisdom and tall tales or good stories that will tickle your fantasy.

I your writer, Neal B. Whittaker, has spent many days and hours in this store.

(At this point Neal encourages us to turn from page one to page two)

He goes on to say the readers will learn all about the many things that are true and did happen at the store.

Behind the store we had a big garage with an ice house below. We took big trucks to E. C. Tussey's pond to cut blocks of ice. The ice on the pond was 14" thick. We stored the ice in the ice house with lots of straw to sell when summer came.

One day C. W. Whitaker told us that an old car in the driveway must be moved. We pushed it into the big ice house Of course, all the ice had been sold. I did help push it into the ice house.

We also had a chicken coop. We bought hens and roosters and put them in the coop. The produce man came once per week to buy our stock of produce.

"author's note" To clarify the following sketch for readers who may not be familiar with the practice of country stores purchasing live chickens. People would bring in chickens, be paid in cash for them and some customers would volunteer to take the hens or roosters to the coop for Mable, Neal's mother.

The boys, who hung around the store would get a big hen from the stores coop, bring it in the front door to sell to mother Mable, and volunteer to take it to the coop. Soon, someone else would bring in a big rooster to sell to mother Mable and take it to the coop for her. When the day was over, each one of the boys gave mother her money back. They were honest, just having a lot of fun.

The next story happened to be a favorite of Neal's wife, Dorothy who was recently deceased at the time of this writing. Neal writes, "near the store we had a big grist mill where people would bring corn to be ground into meal or chicken scratch. One Wednesday night Mom and Dad went to prayer meeting at the Salem Christian Church. Upon returning, Dad noticed the mill door was open. He checked the door and someone inside said, "hello Doc." My father was called Doc, I never did know why. Dad looked a little closer to see a neighbor man, who was drunk and had fallen into the big meal tub with his feet sticking up and could not get out.

Inside this big store we had a small radio that had fallen off the shelf and had broken its outer case. At times when it would stop playing, the lazy loafers would not want to get up and fix it so it's playing would resume. The loafers would pick up a potato and throw it at the radio. When they would hit it, the Midday Merry-go-round from W. H. O. X. Knoxville, Tennessee with Lowell Blanchard was loud and clear. One potato saved the day, now back to the all time favorite past time, the checker game.

One day a customer asked Dad the price of matches. Dad told him a nickel a box or three boxes for a quarter. The customer said, "might as well get three boxes, we are always out at home."

On one occasion someone wanted to buy one glove. Dad said one is twenty five cents or two for seventy five cents. The man replied, "might as well buy both of them, my other hand gets cold also.

After work on the farms, loafers would come to the store after supper. One night, about 9:00 P. M. the front door opened and in came Esau Powell and his wife Velva. They were carrying the following items. Esau was carrying a guitar and a step ladder, while Velva was carrying a well chain and a slop jar. Then Velva said, "we are moving and it's about to kill me."

In the next segment, Neal offers a prologue to his narrative. He begins by saying, "this is a true story as the others are true also. However, this one is my favorite, I was there when it happened. I have told it every place I have traveled. John Patton, auctioneer, asked me to tell it to him. It is a classic."

My Dad decided to build a small office in a rear corner of the store. We had a roll-top desk and chair and a big combination safe inside. My Dad had a half brother, Raymond Howard. I weighed him one day and he weighed 320 pounds. He wanted to look inside to watch the work. When the job was finished and Uncle Raymond got up to leave, he could not get through the door, so Dad had to take the wall down to get him out. Again, Neal reiterates, "I was there also."

Our store was large and cold with only one stove or heater. Our store was sixty foot long and forty foot wide. It had a big back room which was not heated. Here we kept our soda pop, feed, rugs and kerosene tank. We hung rolls of bologna on big hooks. At times it would have mold on it. We would bring it inside, take a clean rag and vinegar, wipe it clean and just keep slicing. No one ever got sick.

One winter day a good friend, Nelson Davis, came through the front door and yelled, "this is going to be a pop buster tonight," so we carried all the pop into the warmer room.

My Dad went to Weck's Auction in Lexington each week. He would take his big truck with cattle racks to bring home his purchases. He bought roll-top desks for six and eight dollars each, and cane bottom chairs for 25 cents each. On one occasion he bought a couch and chair for ten dollars and displayed them in the store. One day a lady came in to look at the couch. Dad told her he was lucky to find such a good couch. When she asked the price, Dad told her the couch alone was thirty dollars. Mildred, Neal's little sister observing the transaction said, "thirty dollars, you told mother you just paid ten dollars for all of it." My Dad told Mildred to go to her mother. The lady bought the couch for thirty dollars. My Dad said, "thank you" and smiled.

As business dictates, we would get a bill of lading for the goods we bought. We hung them on a wire hook until paid. As we paid the bills we would have to file them away for safe keeping. We had a big banana box to place the paid bills in. My brother, Nelson, would put the bill into the box and press them down tight with his foot. Filing proper.

People came by way of horse and buggy, sled, wagon, walking or riding a horse to shop. Mrs. Harold Hendren came to shop and we put her purchases into her buggy. She and her daughter, Lenora Boone Hendren drove from the store. Lenora was driving the horse, or pony. As they left, Lenora kept looking back at me standing on the store's front porch. She pulled the reins so tight to the left, the buggy, groceries and mother Hattie Lee ran over the bank in front of Mother and Dad's home. Hattie Lee told Boone, "as soon as we get home, I'll take a limb to wear you out if you think you are courting Neal Burnam Whitaker."

Of course we received letters that we owed for things bought. Dad looked them over and added them up to a total. He said, "I don't have the money now," so this is what he did. He put a check in an envelope for each vendor he owed and sent them to the wrong address. I asked him why he did it that way? He told me when they all send them back to me I will have the money by then. He did, and all was paid in full. Honest, but skillful was my Dad.

In our vicinity we had a group of people, or families named Long. They were all honest people. One day, William McKinley Long bought a refrigerator from us. He lived in a small rental house on Silver Creek in the Crow Valley area. One day I told my brother-in-law, Roy Patterson, we needed to deliver the purchase to the customer. When we arrived at Long's little house, I backed up to the door to unload. I asked him where to put the merchandise and he said, "in the kitchen." I told him the heat from the stove would make it run more and he said, "O. K., just put it in the other room." With a dolly we put it where instructed. I looked around and told Long, "there is no plug-in in here." He came in wearing big four buckle overshoes with mud on them. He took the cord and looked at it, with his foot he kicked a hole in the wall and said, "stick it through there, I think it will work."

"author's note" Departing Neal's contribution briefly, I recently discussed this incident with William McKinley's son, Lewis Ray Long, who resides in Berea, Kentucky. He said, "that sounds like something the old man would do." He also shared he later came into possession of the refrigerator, which was a Crosley, and it remained in his Berea home for many years performing perfectly.

We bought such items as furs and rabbits. We hung the rabbits in the big back room. We paid ten (10) cents each for the rabbits and sold them to a Mr. Winkler from Lexington for fifteen (15) cents each. Mr. Winkler came in a big van to get the rabbits. We started stacking the dead rabbits from the front of the van all the way to our back room where they were being loaded. Our stack of rabbits was about two or three feet wide and about three feet high and about forty foot long. We counted them and Mr. Winkler paid us in cash and was on his way a fortunate, well pleased man. He later peddled them on Water Street in Lexington for about twenty five (25) cents each.

At this point Neal makes an observation with the following comment.

What's in the future? Next week, more dead rabbits and Mr. Winkler.

Behind our store there was a two car garage with a post in the center. One night my brother, Harry Dean Whitaker drove Dad's car somewhere. Upon returning home I think he hit a hog on the way back. He drove into the garage and turned the steering wheel to a dead left. Next morning, Dad was going to a meeting in Richmond. He backed the car out quickly striking the post hard enough to tear off the fender that Harry Dean had placed back on the car after the encounter with the hog.

Neal closes this segment on Whitaker's Store by signing,
                                        Col. Neal B. Whittaker

Whitaker's Store

Col. Neal Burnam Whittaker

MORE COUNTRY STORES

In the previous segment, Neal Burnam has allowed his memory to meander back to the time when he actively participated in the day-to-day activities of his family's country store. In his next contribution, he begins at the Kentucky River and provides a concise description of the many country stores which existed during the period of which he writes, all the way to and including Kirksville.

As is common in many of Neal's hand written articles, he begins with an introduction to expand upon the ingredients which go into the telling of a good story.

He begins with," The story you are about to read is truly logical." As you read, you will allow your mind to wander to the good old days of your childhood. To be able to compare everything, and dream as you may, as we try to tell about a real country store. Around what we think arose some of the finest humor and motherly wisdom one could find, just a storehouse full of real fun as we can see. I was just thinking, some of the nearby stores are the main part of our subject.

Near the foothills of the Cumberlands, in the bluegrass of Kentucky, we travel to find the scene of this story. This place is Poosey Ridge. Poosey Ridge is located nine to fifteen miles northwest of Richmond, Kentucky in Madison County. As we travel from Richmond on highway #52 to #595, or the Barnes Mill Road, we find Kirksville, Round Hill, Cottonburg, Edenton and to the flowing Kentucky River. This is north of villages mentioned above, and the end of Poosey Ridge Road, once called The Kirksville-Kentucky River Turnpike.

At this point, Neal begins his history of the many Poosey Ridge country stores.

A gentleman in Lexington told me a Mr. Olee ran a store at the river. I believe Noland Warren ran this store for awhile. I was never in this store; and a house was nearby. Going south up the road we come to the New Road. A short distance beyond, Wilbert Smith ran a small country store.

I have heard it said someone went to George Thomas Hill's store nearby to get groceries which were put in a large paper sack. It began to rain and the bag got wet. The person or persons stopped at Smith's store to get a new sack to put the items in. Mr. Smith, an easy going, kind hearted man said, "yes, come on in out of the rain, I'll re-sack them for you at no charge." A good man to know.

Back to the main road we stop at George Thomas Hill's store. There were many different people who ran this store. I think Margie Warren once operated this store as well as some lady who told the customers to put the soft-drink bottles back where they got them after consuming the contents. So, after drinking the pop, the customers put the empties back into the cooler. At this location was a United States Post Office. One day while they were working inside the store, a gentleman told me they moved the Post office across the road and put it up in a big tree. I don't know if this is true or not. Don't quote me for sure.

These little stores were close to each other. Connie Davis ran a small store up the road from Hill's. Keep in mind, he also made furniture along with his store.

Soon we arrive at the Mitch Collins home-place. In front of the old home is a small building. Lois, Mitch's son ran a small store. Now we arrive at the big store. A. B. Clark bought this store from a Mr. Reagan in 1903. Andrew B. Clark died in 1938 and was buried in Mt. Hebron cemetery in Garrard County. The story goes Bob Chandler bought a horse collar without a pad from Clark's store. He put it on the horse. The fact it did not have a pad under the collar when he worked the horse cause sores. Chandler took the collar back to Clark, who inspected it and took a pocket knife, cut it up and said, "now rub."

At A. B. Clark's store, people would bring produce to trade for goods he sold. Clark then raised a trap door to drop the hens and roosters into a large pen below. At Clark's store he had Russell Barlow pocket knives on a board hanging on a nail. If he took one off to sell it to someone and happened to drop it on the floor, he would just let it lay. I think they were fifteen (15) cents and Twenty five (25) cents retail. Clark had a man from Jessamine County to conduct an auction of lots of items. He had a large back room full of shoes.

In the year 1937, A. B. Clark took sick and was not able to operate his store. He hired Russell Whitaker to close out the big store. Many times have I been in this big store. Russell was a brother to my father, Creighton. I have already told you about his store.

Squire Hendren ran a small store at the Cora Duncan place. Uncle Squire, as we called him, carried the mail on horseback. I remember this so well.

Will Snyder ran a country store where Jack Land and John Will Teater lived. My Dad told me he took rabbits to Will Snyder's store to sell for ten (10) cents each, enough to buy a cheap bicycle.

Near the top of Pilant, or Sled Branch Road, Joe Burton ran a leather and harness shop. Joe was a cripple and he walked, sort of, on his hands. He was Richard Burton's son. He had a small stock of goods available to meet customer needs.

As we pass the Salem Christian Church on the east side, we come to the R. E. "Dick" Burgess store. I was not inside this store too much. I was so young, mother didn't want me to stray away too far. Dick Burgess had a store full of things people needed.

Luther Reynolds had a set up one does not see too often. He had a grist mill on one end , a country store in the middle and a blacksmith shop on the other end. These three businesses were all under one roof. At Luther's place you could get your corn ground, get groceries or have your horse or mule shod. All under one roof.

When I was a child on the Burton Lane, someone told me a Steve Hill ran a store where Steve Agee's garage was located. Vernon Stocker owns it now. I also heard during a wind storm it was blown across the road into a field. I am not too sure about this.

I know where Joe Bob Hendren ran a small country store. Ethel Collins and her two boys, Johnny and Billy Mitchell owns this property. This is where the big barn fell in. If you go to the north corner of the big barn to the road, this store set on a bee-line to the corner of the barn. It was near the Poosey Methodist Church, the Ferrill Cemetery and the Arch Ferrill home place where Lena Vincent lived.

Clayton Reynolds ran a country store in front of the Poosey school. He had a post office here at this place. Clayton was a nephew of the afore-mentioned Luther Reynolds. Clayton lived at the Bob Whitaker home place where large crowds could be seen at the parties to listen to country music at its best. Mr. and Mrs. Whitaker always told us to come back soon, and we did.

Eb Moberly and his wife, Sally B., ran a store at the next location. My father actually purchased this store. I was very young at the time, and it was here Lewis Ward sat me on a nail keg to cut off my curls which were hanging down, while mother sat and cried.

So here we are at C. W. Whitaker's first country store. Elzie Calico owned the property, so my father paid him rent. We had a full line of groceries, hardware, clothing etc. Here is where I got my nickname, "Coonie." Eb Moberly had a pet coon which lay inside the show case where the candy was displayed.

There was a boy named Agee who came to the store. This boy had some firecrackers he wanted to trade. When I asked him what he wanted for them, he said, " a big hand-full of that Christmas candy inside the store." When I went to get the candy, my father asked, "what's that in your candy," I answered, "Eb's old coon." A big crowd was at the store, so they started calling me "Coonie." My wife's people in Garrard County are the only ones today who call me "Coonie."

I will make a brief departure from Neal's chronicle of Poosey Ridge country stores in order to insert some personal knowledge of Eb's and Sally B's menagerie. When I read Neal's account of the Moberly's pet coon, the memories came flooding back to when my family told a very similar story. The story which circulated in my family for many years was on this wise. When the Moberly's ran this store, not only did they have "Coonie", but also a rather large white tomcat they called "Snowy". The two animals seemed to co-exist amiably within the walls of the store building. One fateful day, however, when the Moberly's were away, the two pets entered into an altercation which elevated to such violence each participant died as a result of injuries inflicted one upon the other. After this sad event, when Sally B. told the story she would always end by saying "Coonie killed Snowy and Snowy killed Coonie."

The next store to be visited on our journey southward toward Kirksville, is the enterprise of Miss Emma Sowers, who's business bore the same name. She also operated a post office out of this location which became known as the Cottonburg post office. The location of this facility going north toward the river, is a sharp turn to the right after passing the home(at that time)of James "Jim" Rhodus on the left. The store was also on the left after passing the curve near the Hendren School. To the south of the store was a road known as the Marg Turner Branch Road which led to Dry Branch. Miss Sowers was a sister to Mrs. Alfred "Mary" Malear and Mrs. Jim "Lucy" Rhodus. Neal B. reports Miss Emma was a former school teacher in Crow Valley near Corinth Christian Church.

At this juncture in his narrative, Neal arrives at what we will refer to as the big store at Cottonburg which was erected in 1904 and operated by the Whitakers from 1924 until 1974. Neal makes it clear W. E. "Bill" Whitaker who ran the store from 1924 to 1936 was not a relative.

The following is repetitive of the store's history as related in the original "Hills That Beckon."

Built in 1904 by Robert Long for a son-in-law, Les Cotton
Who operated the store from 1904 to 1918.

Millard Campbell 1918-1919
Cecil Broadus 1919-1924
W. E. Whitaker 1924-1936
C. W. Whitaker 1936-1947
C. W. & Nelson Whitaker 1947-1954
Neal B. & Nelson Whitaker 1954- 1974

In this segment relating to Whitaker's store, Neal highlights many of the same details and events which occurred in his previous reminisces of the old family store. Therefore, this author will edit and choose information which has not been previously presented.

In olden times there was a drawer under the top of the counter for money. This was called the till. It had a bell on it and the bell would ring each time it was opened.

It was told someone went to the store and Creighton was trying to think of a customer he had sold a pair of boots to on credit. Creighton reportedly said, "oh well, if he don't pay me his feet will be dry."

This store provided marble rings, horse shoe pitching, country music and card games. Most people just waited on themselves. They would lay the money on the counter and leave.

At this juncture, Neal pays tribute to his father, of which much has already been said. He continues by saying, sociable, friendly, accommodating, good story teller, well read bible man, God fearing, teacher, farmer, merchant, auctioneer, peacemaker, trader, fisherman and traveler. This is the "C. W." or Creighton Whitaker who operated the large country store at Cottonburg.

As this account of Whitaker's store continues to unfold, Neal waxes poetic as he describes the day -to-day activity.

A wonderful place was the country store, the kind we used to see. Where we carried our baskets of new laid eggs, to trade them off for tea. For sugar and salt and laundry soap, for needles and nuts and nails. For muslin and matches and underwear, and buckets and pans and pails.

People liked to trade at the old country store. Farmers came in flocks, with rolls of money so fresh and new, to barter it off for socks. For candy and cakes and chicken feed, for shovels and shoes and beans, for indigo and sapolio, and molasses from New Orleans.

It was great to work at the country store with the staple line of goods, where overalls and hand-me-downs were kept with the breakfast foods. With home grown foods and calico, with goods for the gingham frocks. With plows and pumps and garden tools along with bolts and locks.

If you have never dealt at an old country store, you have missed a lot you see, and the folks that did will bear me out, I'm sure all will agree. A wonderful place was the country store as in the days of old, mark it sold.

In Neal's next depiction of life at the old country store, in his own mind he discloses how some in the community actually scrutinize the merchant.

When a merchant arises too late, he is running his store in a careless way and is soon going broke. When he arises early, he is trying to sell you something so he can soon retire.

When he stays home to take care of his business , he doesn't get out to associate with society enough. When he goes someplace, he should be home taking care of his business.

When he buys a new car, he has beat his customers and they have paid for it. When he drives an old truck, he has made a failure and can't afford one.

When he is friendly, he is building his business. When he is not friendly, he wasn't cut out to be a merchant.

When he does not attend church, he is a lost man. When he goes to church, he is overloaded and trying to sell something.

When he doesn't have what you want, his stock has run down. When he displays bargains, they must be ruining on him.

When the store is too hot, he has made a big sale. When the loafers get cold, he is a bad fireman.

When his wife helps in the store, she is looking bad. When she doesn't help him, she thinks she is too good for those he serves.

When his clothes are dirty, he should clean up. When he cleans up, he must be going someplace.

When he has no spittoons, he should buy some. When he
buys some, they never hit them.

Neal continues buy saying, I can remember when goods like
coffee, tea, pepper, salt, soda crackers, soda, beans, prunes, peaches,
apricots, vinegar, tobacco, rice, lard, molasses and fish all came in
bulk. So the early balance scales and liquid measures were in our
store.

A lot of merchandise hung from the ceiling. Brooms were
hung to a circular hanging rack. We had an old tobacco cutter
where you would insert a slab and cut off a plug. Scoops and
forks are all gone nowadays.

Once again, Neal lapses into lyrical license as he attempts to
describe the memories which have become so much a part of his
life.

So I have a pleasant memory, hard to locate anymore, A
really true and genuine old fashioned country store.
Oh: the modern stores are stylish with their bright goods
on the shelf, and the wagons you push along while waiting
on yourself.
But sometimes I get to wishing that I could return once
more, to unearth some new surprises in a real old country
store.

We realize there is so much to be said about Whitaker's store,
and we rest assured that later writers can, and probably will go more
into detail about the old cluttered, leisurely way of operating a large
country store. Better ways of selling goods have come along. None,
however, can take the place in our mind of Whitaker's store as a social
institution. True, it was a store, but it was also a tradition which Neal
says he will ever hold dear in his remembrances of things past.

Next in line we find O. E. Click's store which is not far from
Whitaker's store. O. E. Click came to Poosey about 1920. He was a

fine man. His wife's name was Bertha. Neal ventures a guess that the Clicks came from Jackson County, Kentucky. They had two sons and one daughter. Hershel, Thurston and Evelyn. Neal adds Evelyn was a lovely lady. Joe Marshall Masters purchased this store from Mr. and Mrs. Vernon Stocker. This store is closed as of this writing.

In Round Hill, Jasper Wylie ran a big store. Today it is closed: someone pushed it back about fifty feet to make it into a storage shed.

J. H. Estes ran a big store in Round Hill. His son's were Joe and Doug, both deceased. This Estes family were large land owners and people of wealth.

In front of Estes' store was the E. C. Tussey and John L. Whitlock store. Many People operated this store. Neal Burnam himself, bought this store in 1945 and operated it until 1953. He then built a home near Whitaker's store in Cottonburg. As was referred to, many people managed and/ or operated this store. First, there was the J. W. Purkey and Estes store with steps on each side of the front of the building. Later a new building was built at ground level. The following individuals ran this store at varying intervals. Some of them were, Robert Cox, Todd Stocker, Robert Taylor, Ed Land, Fred Prewitt and Burnam Miller Jr. Neal B. Whittaker purchased the store from John L. Whitlock in 1945 Neal says this store, which he operated until 1953, was a success for him.

Neal shares some personal feelings surrounding this store as he describes the sad event of this store burning about August 16, 1966. He goes on to say someone called to tell him the store was burning. He drove to Round Hill to watch it burn. T. J. Griggs, who Neal describes as his best helper was there also. In Neal's own words, "we both stood and cried."

Neal, in his lighthearted approach, advises us to travel on to Kirksville. He begins with, Charles Wagers ran a good store here, which he later sold to Reather Murphy. Reather sold it to Willie B.

York. Neal say's he sold this store at auction for Mr. York. Neal goes on to say he bought a fire proof safe from Murphy and sold it to the Porter Memorial Church in Lexington.

Directly in front of Murphy's store, John Smith ran a small store which was on the S. E. Wheeler property.

Jess Blakeman ran a big store in Kirksville. We used to go to this store from the High School. While there, I noticed a little add on the top of a big showcase that read, " a good thing to do is to work with the construction gang and not the wrecking crew." Jess Blakeman had a cat which stayed in the store at night. A light was left on during the night, and every morning when Jess opened the front door, the cat would stand erect on its hind legs and pull the string to turn the light off. Neal emphasizes the cat story by saying, "this is the truth." The lodge was upstairs over Blakeman's store.

Harry Potts operated a general store in Kirksville about 1925. Neal was not too clear exactly where this store was located.

Bill Hubble's father had a small store in Kirksville, which included a post office.

Neal shares a bit of local history with the following comments. Samuel Kirkendall, a Kirksville merchant, recorded a deed in 1847 changing the name of the village of Centerville to Kirksville.

Now we have come to the end of a much loved documentation about the country stores on Poosey Ridge Road. It has not been our intention to leave one person, or his or her store, from this writing. However, one has come to mind. At Bradshaw Mill, off Poosey Ridge Road to Dry Branch Road and down to paint Lick Creek, I know in 1945 Mike Bogie ran a store here. A Mr. Focus ran this store as well as Harlan Reynolds. Adding some personal information relative to Neal's reminiscence, my family moved to Dry Branch in the fall of 1942, and Mike Bogie was operating the store at that time. Mike must have run the store for several years.

Neal ends this enlightening history of Poosey Ridge country stores with a few personal thoughts of his own. He wishes to communicate to all who reads what he has written just how much he has enjoyed and appreciated the opportunity to be able to share his precious memories from the past.

Neal writes, "being raised in a large country store most of my life, and being owner or co-owner for thirty five years with my brother, Nelson Ray Whitaker, deceased, is one reason I have enjoyed this so much. My good wife of fifty five years, Dorothy Clark Whittaker, has been a great help in every way she could. I just want to thank her, and to thank all our customers that traded at our country store. Thank you! Thank you again.

Written by Col. Neal B. Whittaker
March 6, 2001"

Neal lost his beloved Dorothy in January, 2008 after sixty two years of marriage.

The next segment will be the beginning of the end of Neal Burnam's much appreciated account of the way things used to be, and are no more. Neal mailed me a copy of his Poosey Ridge Trivia several years ago with instructions, "not for publication at all". When I began to toy with the idea of writing a sequel to "The Hills That Beckon," I asked Neal if I might be able to include his trivia since I saw nothing offensive in its content. In a letter from him dated December 4, 2005, he extended to me his written permission. Along with the hand written trivia questions and answers, there was also a cover letter explaining why, and the need for this venture. The subsequent presentation will begin with the cover letter followed by "Poosey Ridge Trivia."

"This Poosey Ridge trivia was first thought of by Col. Neal B. Whittaker of Richmond, Kentucky. It was written which he held from memory alone. It is written with no intention of what-so-ever to be insulting to one person in any way. I just had the idea it would be fun to record a few facts about Poosey Ridge, KY, the land I love dearly and the place I was born July 25, 1920.

Just love to talk about the people I love.

Not for publication at all.

By: Col. Neal B. Whittaker"

POOSEY RIDGE TRIVIA

Q. What happened November 28, 1941?
A. John Warren drowned

Q. What is last house name?
A. This is it.

Q. Who was Mr. O'Lee ?
A. Ran a big store at the river.

Q. Where is the big sink hole?
A. On Noland Warren's farm.

Q. Who had lots of cats and catwalk?
A. Myrtle Warren.

Q. Who was shot and loaded onto a horse?
A. William Cook, a counterfeiter in 1879.

Q. Who was Jesse Alverson?
A. A black man rescued from his home in 1890 when Silver Creek was at flood stage.

Q. Who fell from a peach tree and died in 1926?
A. William Edward Cook(young boy)

Q. Who was aunt Dood Smith?
A. Bessie Hughes mother.

Q. Who taught his first school at Sallee School?
A. C. W. "Creighton" Whitaker.+

Q. What was Geedie Hill's full name?
A. George Thomas Hill, Edenton merchant.

Q. Who was Needie and Pokie Reynolds?
A. Luther and Allie Reynolds's sisters.

Q. Where did Monkey Tail Warren hold a revival?
A. Connie Davis' little work shop.

This one needs a little explaining. His name was Harold Warren and was a native of Jessamine County. He was a preacher and it was said he was born with a "pump knot" on the end of his tail bone and was called Monkey Tail. It must have been noticeable. He knew people called him that and it was O. K. with him. He preached in a small church in Poosey from time to time.

Q. Where is the Reagan Lane?
A. Near A. B. Clark's home place.

Q. Who was a merchant from 1903 to 1938?
A. Andrew B. Clark. Married a Stone and Onstott lady.

Q. Who learned to walk under a dining room table?
A. Neal B. Whittaker and Carl Chandler at Bob Chandler's.

Q. Who ran a store and carried mail on horseback?
A. Squire Hendren.

Q. Who made farm gates and sold them?
A. Jack Warner.

Q. Who carried John Will Teater from a fire?
A. Virgil "Jack" Land.

Q. Who had eight sons and two daughters?
A. Shirley Land.

Q. Why was Gunner Field so named?
A. John Land worked on guns.

Q. Why was Buck Hollow so named?
A. Buck Lowery family.

Q. Who was seen wallowing in a pond with hogs?
A. Abraham Burton's son.

Q. Who was president of The Kentucky River Turnpike (Poosey)?
A. Conrad Chrisman, lived in Kirksville.

Q. Where was the big marble ring in the road?
A. On the New Road in Poosey?

Q. Who had ten children each to count only sixteen?
A. Robert A. Whitaker - six by Miss Agee.
-four by Harriet Howard Harriet six by Marion Howard -four by
Robert A. Whitaker, my Grand pap and -Grandmother Whitaker. Six
each when married, then four more of which C. W. Whitaker was one
of four. Got it? O. K.!

Q. Where is Stand Around?
A. Wylie Schoolhouse on New Road.

Q. Who carried rock from a creek bed for a rock fence?
A. Lurrie Whitaker on Sled Branch road.

Q. Who drew a civil war pension in Poosey?
A. Jake Teater.

Q. Where is Bear Wallow Church?
A. Salem Christian Church.

Q. Where is the Harris Hendren house?
A. Home of Lafayette Howard and Rastus Stipes.

Q. Who had seven sons?
A. Fred Howard, died Sept. 30, 1933...…49 years old.

Q. Who was one of the oldest men in Poosey?
A. Perry Warren, 96 years of age.

Q. Who taught a night school in Poosey?
A. Mrs. Elzie(Bessie)Calico. (Neal B. attended it.)

Q. When did the Poosey School burn?
A. December 16, 1932.

Q. Who had a white beard to his waist?
A. Elisha Warren, died 1926.

Q. Who planted corn all day and died the next day at 10:00 A. M.
A. Neal's grandfather, George Teater, Neal helped, 50 cents per day.

Q. Who was eating peaches in the shade and died the next day?
A. Ollie Tudor.

Q. Who built the Ethel Collins house?
A. Dr. W. K. Price, 1931 or 32.

Q. Who from Poosey was county Judge in 1920?
A. Dr. W. K. Price.

Q. Whose colt fell into a well in 1926?
A. Rice Warner's.

Q. Who pulled it out with a Buick automobile?
A. C. W. Whitaker. Neal say's, "I was there."

Q. Who went down into the well to put a harness on the colt?
A. Otis Ward.

Q, Who climbed into an old oil tank in Poosey?
A. Moss Agee, James Cotton and Noland Warren.

Q. Who closed the top on the oil tank?
A. Russell Ross Sr.

Q. Who played country music at the bottom of a cistern?
A. Bob Whitaker and son's, Robert Price, Frazier and Garnett, at a beef club in front of Poosey School.

Q. Where was the Hendren school house?
A. Mrs. William Clay "Duff" Masters home today.
This was true at the time of Neal's writing.

Q. Where was buggy put on top of a garage?
A. C. W. Whitaker's first store. The Elzie Calico property.

Q. Who scared off officers with a black poker?
A. Mrs. William Cook in 1879, to protect her husband who was a known counterfeiter in Poosey.

Q. Who fell off his wagon to die the next day?
A. Garnett Masters, October8, 1929.

Q. Who are the four widowed sisters in Poosey?
A. Ethel Collins, Carrie McCully, Stella Davis, and Ann Masters. One sister, Mable Prather, also a widow living in Richmond. This was also true at the time of Neal's writing.

Q. What did Long Jim Vincent build in 1931 and 1932?
A. Stone fence at the Poe Coy farm.

Q. Where did Bartlett Tubs live in Poosey?
A. On the Helen Thompson farm on Burton Lane.

Q. Who had five sons and one daughter/five daughters and one son?
A. Neighbors, C. W. Whitaker/Jesse Clark.

Q. Where did Lena Vincent come from?
A. Nobody knows.

Q. Where did Lena Vincent tell C. W. Whitaker to unload the six ton of coal from truck?
A. Through the front window into the big front room. Neal helped scoop it out.

Q. What were the names of the minister and artist at Salem Christian Church?
A. Railsback and Boone, preached and drew pictures.

Q. Who rode two horses up the steps of Salem Christian Church?
A. I think I know. "no comment."

Q. Who was sleeping in a folding bed when it folded up?
A. Raymond Howard and wife Jennie.

Q. Who won a box of candy at Bob Whitaker's party for making the ugliest face, and said he wasn't playing?
A. Arthur "Prod" Tudor.

Q. Who said, "he has shot the preacher" at Robert Clark's funeral at Salem Cemetery?
A. Alvin Howard.

Q. Who was feeding a hay baler with his foot, to get it crushed by the roller?
A. A black man working for C. W. Whitaker on the Bogie farm. Neal
B. was the closest to him. Year was 1930.

Q. Where was the Forest Marsh/Will Snyder store?
A. John Will Teater or Virgil Land home.

Q. Who was the crippled shoe cobbler?
A. Little Joe Burton.

Q. From whose long white beard did a magician shake a pan of quarters into and where?
A. Poosey School, from Elisha Warren's beard.

Q. How many roads led from Poosey Ridge road to Wheeler Branch road?
A. Four: Perry Warren house, Fred Howard's barn, Burton Lane entrance and Johnny Moton Warren garage.

Q. Who from Salem Christian Church was baptized in a big chair?
A. Ed Warren at Joe Long's pond at Round Hill.

Q. Whose horse's tail did the calves chew off?
A. C. W. Whitaker's, while teaching at Sallee School.

Q. Who asked Bill Long for direction in Poosey?
A. John Dillinger.

Q. What was old Mammy Hill's name?
A. Liza Jane Brunfield Hill. Her husband, Johnnie Hill.

Q. Who built a large house in Poosey and died three days after moving into it?
A. Brud Davis. (the Fred Howard house)

Q. Who won the Victrola by lucky ticket in 1930 at W. E. "Bill" Whitaker's store?
A. Dan Long. (Franklin Whitaker drew the winning ticket)

Q. Who is the only boy from Poosey Ridge to marry the sheriff's daughter?
A. Neal Burnam Whittaker.

Q. Who had eight girls and six boys in Cottonburg?
A. Wm "Bill" Taylor

Q. Whose farm in Garrard County produced a two headed calf?
A. C. W. Whitaker's.

Q. When was REA turned on for Poosey Ridge?
A. 1939.

Q. Where was the quarry for rock used on Poosey Ridge road?
A. Wolford Agee property, top of Dry Branch road.

Q. Who died in Poosey between plow handles?
A. John Collins, Mitch Collins Great Grand Dad.

Q. Who sold his cow twice to the same man in one day?
A. C. W. Whitaker sold Abe Burton a cow for $90.00, bought the cow back for $100.00. Sold her back to Burton for $110.00.

Q. Name some men of great distinction in Poosey.
A. Colonel Ward, General Schooler, Duke Bellamy, Earl Hendren, Major Hamm and Colonel Burton.

Q. Who did DeFord Bailey, on The Grand Ole Opry, dedicate the Fox Chase(harmonica) on Saturday night?
A. Bill Long of Duck Branch road, a big fox hunter.

Q. Who carried a long stick, walking along Poosey Ridge road?
A. Blind Walter Tudor.

Q. Where is the Arch Ferrill house, and when was it built?
A. Perry Warren home, built in 1840.

Q. Whose car was rooted by hogs, rolled into a hollow?
A. Rufus Blakeman's, at Oscar Hendren's house.

Q. Who told his wife, "your children and my children are playing with our children?"
A. Robert A. Whitaker to his wife Harriet.

POOSEY POTPOURRI

The following portion of this narrative with the strange sounding title is explained in this manner. The word potpourri can mean assortment, mixture or miscellaneous. This is exactly how this next segment will be developed, consisting of brief entries connected to people and/or activities associated with Poosey Ridge. A good portion of the content is taken from clippings found in my grandmother's scrapbook which were acquired from "The Richmond Daily Register" beginning in the early nineteen forties. Unfortunately, my grandmother did not include the date of the articles. I believe I have used the analogy elsewhere in this narrative, but researching this old scrapbook, which is approaching seventy (70) years of age, with its brittle pages and wrinkled and faded articles and photographs is akin to researching the "Dead Sea Scrolls."

PRIVATE SCRIVNER WOUNDED IN ACTION

"Pvt. Kenneth Dow Scrivner was wounded in action in Germany on Sept. 20, according to a message received from the war department by his parents, Mr. And Mrs. Ballard Scrivner. He is now in a hospital in England. He has been awarded the Purple Heart. Private Scrivner has been in the army since May, 1943. He has served in England, France, Belgium and Germany. He was among the first invasion forces in France."

*Author's note: I personally knew Kenneth and his parents when my family lived in the area.

The next offering showed a type of banner which presented an American Flag with the words "With The Armed Forces," with a photograph of two young men standing side by side and appeared to be dressed in white T-shirts. Below the photo were the words,

"CPL. GLENMORE TAYLOR(left)AND SGT. FRANK TAYLOR(above) sons of Mrs. William Taylor, route one Richmond, who recently met in the Philippines and spent six days together. Corporal Taylor, the husband of Mrs. Madaline Burgess Taylor, North Second Street, Richmond, entered the service on May 4, 1944. Sergeant Taylor was inducted on July 4, 1944. The boys had not seen each other for six months prior to their unexpected meeting."

*Author's note: There was extensive coverage given the Taylor family in the book, "The Hills That Beckon." Mr. And Mrs. William Taylor were the parents of fourteen (14) children. As of this writing only Glenmore remains.

The headlines say, serving with the armed forces, and a photograph below showing two soldiers in full dress uniform. The message beneath the photo says in bold letters, BROTHERS MEET OVERSEAS

"Cpl. Harlan Reynolds (left) and Cpl. Clayton Reynolds, sons of Allie Reynolds, Edenton, recently met and spent a seven-day furlough together in England. Cpl. Harlan Reynolds has been in the service 30 months and has been overseas since July, and Cpl. Clayton Reynolds has been in the service 27 months and overseas since July."

There was a rather small notice in the Register relative to two Poosey Ridge residents who were serving overseas.

Pvt. Russell Dean Prather has arrived safely in France, according to word received by his parents, Mr. and Mrs. Bert Prather. Pfc. Neal B. Whittaker is now in Germany, according to word received by his parents, Mr. and Mrs. C. W. Whitaker. Private Whittaker has served in England, France and Belgium He writes his parents that he is well and happy and will see them soon.

*Author's note: Mr. And Mrs. Bert Prather, their two sons, Russell Dean and Cecil were our neighbors while living on Turner's Ridge. There has already been much said about Neal B. in this writing.

A photo showing three soldiers dressed in uniforms. The message under the photo reads,

THREE MADISON COUNTY MEN now stationed in Berlin. Reading from left to right Cpl. Nelson Whitaker, Pfc. Richard A. Webb and Cpl. Harold Richardson. These three local boys share the same apartment in the German capitol.

*Author's note. I believe Nelson was the only Poosey Ridge resident among the three. But then, I could be wrong.

The following is another example of the many going-away party's given in appreciation by friends and neighbors for young men going into military service as reported by the Register.

FAREWELL PARTY

Miss Helen Tackett entertained with a party Monday night in honor of her brother, Leslie Tackett, who will enter the U. S. Army today. Those present were: The Misses Roberta

70

Long, Helen Ross, Louise Hale, Anna Mae Moody, Emma Ross, Edith Moberly, Adela Rogers, Alene Hatfield, Eunice and Ruth Miller, Helen Margaret, Ruby and Elsie Tackett, Helen and Evelyn Simpson and Lillian Moore; Messers Leslie Tackett, Hubert and Junior Tackett, Dan and G. B. Hale, Junior Teater, Wilson Warren, Clyde Land, Franklin Whitaker, Frank and Harold Taylor, Harold Tackett, Harold and Ernest Rogers, Marvin and Elwood Oliver, Louis and Cecil Short, , Cecil Davis, Bernard Teater, Eldon Sallee, Luther Harrison, Glen Snyder, Junior Miller, Carl Davis, Forster Vaughn, Russell and Vernon Prather, Mason Rhodus, Mr. and Mrs. Burton May, and children, Mrs. Ernest Miller and Mr. and Mrs. Elba Tackett and children.

*Authors note: the Tackett family were our neighbors when living on Dry Branch Road.

The next entry was not taken from the "Register," but somehow has managed to survive several decades. This small document, in some manner, fell into the hands of my aunt, Mary Laura Long Proctor who gave it to me many years ago.

At this point and time I can only guess what prompted the creation of such written material, but the most logical explanation is my uncle, William D. Long, and Kenneth Scrivner were loafing at Whitaker's Store one evening as Neal Burnam was just passing time with a typewriter. It seems Neal used one of the store's order forms for his resolution. The form as well as the message will be duplicated as closely as possible.

Phone Kirksville 38-1/2

C. W. WHITAKER
hardware - dry goods
R. F. D. 1
Richmond, KY

I do hereby agree that I will as one of the newly developed association, better known as the Gang Busters, do all that is ordered for me to do by my president, Mr. Neal Whitaker. We also swear that when all is well that we as blood thirsty men will or ought to do, we will get our armour on and hunt trouble. We are proud of the fact that the people when we or even one of us walk down the street that the one that even think that they may be in our way really do scat. In fact, one man is carrying a wagon on his back from seeing our biggest man on force coming down the street. He was Mr. Dee Long and he really is a blood thirsty man. He can walk a barb wire fence bare footed with a wild cat under each arm looking for a wild cat to jump on. One of our men is Mr, Scrivner and he is really not a lady killer, he just sorta cripples them.

Our motto is shoot first and ask questions later.

SIGN/

Kenneth Dow Scrivner

William D. Long

Mr. did you see that bad looking man pass here???????
N. B. Whitaker.

The two so called blood thirsty men actually signed the resolution.

The following portion will focus on the colloquial wisdom of my great uncle, Samuel "Sam" Long. Sam, a man of limited formal education was self taught in the area of reading, especially the Holy Bible. There were some who considered him a student of the scriptures. I for one have actually heard him preach in a designated church service. There are others, who laughingly would admit to hearing Sam preach on some subjects not found in the scriptures. Sam was born on Moberly Branch, April 24,1900 to Daniel and Laura

Belle Hickam Long. He and his wife, the former Leoma Thomas along with their three daughters, Louise, Clyde and Jewell Dean lived for many years on Moberly Branch, before he bought the property on Poosey Ridge Road from his brother, Les. He became a fixture on Poosey Ridge, being possessed of a keen and alert mind, folk would seek him out to pass the time of day. Whomever he came in contact with, he seemed to have the ability to always leave them laughing. My father, Jim Long admittedly revealed he was closer to Sam than any of his father's brothers. Sam died at age 82 July 26, 1982. It was an honor for me personally to attend his funeral July 29. Sam was also honored to have six good and true men, friends and neighbors, to be casket bearers. They were, Duke Bellamy, Frank Taylor, Clyde Land, Russell Land, W. J. Agee and Junior Rogers.

I have never forgotten the last time I saw Sam to actually be able to talk to him. As was related in the book, "The Hills That Beckon," I had a baby brother to die February 1, 1943. He was laid to rest next to his great grandparents, Daniel and Laura Belle Long in the Gilead Cemetery. Since Sam lived just across the road from the burial site, when he mowed the grass on his parent's graves, he would also mow the grave of my infant brother. Whenever my father was in the area, he would visit Sam and at the same time give him a monetary gift of appreciation for his kindness and consideration. In July of 1979, my parents, my wife Sharon, my daughter Melanie and me traveled to Poosey, and while there visited Sam. While my mother, wife and daughter were inspecting the various monuments in the cemetery, my father and I walked across the road to Sam's house where we found him standing in his front yard. At this time, Sam had already celebrated his seventy ninth birthday in April. He was, in my opinion, still in good physical condition. He was the type of individual who seemed to prefer to be outside as much as possible. In the past, I had always noticed a particular characteristic about Sam. When on a grassy area like a lawn, he would not stand and talk for any length of time, but lie down on the grass with his elbow on the ground and head propped up resting in his hand. He would be looking up in the direction to the person to whom he was talking.

As our conversation began to subside and my father and me were beginning to leave, Sam quickly came to his feet, with considerably less effort than it would take me today. Dad extracted a twenty dollar bill from his wallet and said as he handed it to him, "well Sam, I don't know what we will do when you're gone." Sam quickly replied, "hell!, I ain't going no where, I'll be here." Sadly, Sam did go somewhere, approximately three years from the time he made that statement. Sam, was one of six brothers, which included my grandfather, Les Long. As a child growing up in the area, I saw more of Sam and his family than any of the remainder of my grandfather's brothers. My father has been heard to say many times, Sam was more like his father, Daniel Long, than any of the other brothers.

Another story surrounding Sam, his quick wit, and his ability to disarm verbally many who were engaged in conversation with him. This incident occurred soon after the birth of his third daughter, Jewell Dean. He happened to be at W. E. Whitaker's store where different people were congratulating him upon the arrival of girl number three. One of the well wishers wanted to take the compliment a bit further. This local gentleman was married twelve years before his first child, a son, was born. In a good natured way, he said to Sam, "I'll have to come down to your house and show you how to get a boy." Sam replied, "that will be alright, but I don't want you hanging around there for twelve years."

Johnny Collins, a lifelong resident of Poosey Ridge who probably had known Sam all of his life shared this story. Johnny, his father and others were at a tobacco warehouse in Richmond attempting to sell their crop. He said tobacco was not selling too well this particular year. He noticed Sam walking down one of the isles passing the many skids of tobacco and as he passed he said, "if this tobacco don't start selling any better, I'm going to have to start lawyering."

The following saga has circulated in my family as long as I can remember. Years ago, as I was in the process of writing "The Hills That Beckon" I struggled with the decision whether to include this story at the time, but decided against it. However, since the time the incident occurred is now approaching eighty years, at the time of this writing, I have determined to include it as part of this narrative.

In order to provide some background, the story will begin in this manner. My great grandfather, Daniel Long, had a sister named Martha Jane Long who married Samuel King. They were the parents of three children, William (Bill), Dovie and Jeff. Bill married Mollie Warmouth and one of their issue was William King Jr. who became known as Little Bill King. There were two reasons why he was known as little Bill. One is obvious, being named for his father. The other, he was unfortunately born with a contorted spine which impaired his growth and caused what some might describe as being hunchbacked. I have heard his own relatives comment on the fact his mind was not affected as he was very intelligent. There is a grave marker in the Gilead Cemetery which gives the following information. King, Bill Jr. October 20, 1901 – October 23, 1930. He died three days after his 29th birthday.

As this narrative unfolds, the author wishes to make it clear no disrespect is intended toward members of the King family or the descendants of Sam Long. This story has survived among the members of the Long family for almost eight decades. My grandmother, Annie Long as well as my father James "Jim" Long told this story over and over as long as they lived.

As the story is presented, the author will attempt to be as sensitive as possible in describing the details of what transpired on this late October, 1930 night. Daniel Long, my great grandfather lay dying in his home on Moberly Branch from the effects of pneumonia. There were several people gathered in the home, which was a common practice among families during this period. My father, Jim Long, his mother, Annie Long and Sam Long, Daniel's son, who lived nearby at the time, were representative of some of the individuals present during this difficult and sad experience. I am not sure, other than those mentioned, who were there and who were not. However, before I began detailing the events of this memorable evening, I interviewed my aunt, Mary Laura Long Proctor who was thirteen years old at the time. She remembered the occasion clearly, and said she was not present, but was told of the event and has not forgotten what she was told for what is now close to eighty years.

As the day had come to an end and darkness pervaded the landscape, Sam told Annie he was going to walk across the small hollow to his home for a short time and feed his livestock. He had not been gone long until the ones within the house heard a shot. Annie laughingly remarked, "well, I guess Sam has seen him a haint (haunt)." At night, especially, Sam usually carried a hand gun of some type when traveling any distance. This practice was common at this time in this area. A short time later, there was another shot. After some time had passed Sam came through the kitchen door, and according to Annie, "he was as white as a sheet." She asked him, "Sam, what in the world were you shooting at?" She was not prepared for his answer when he replied, "I guess I have killed Little Bill King."

Sam went on to explain his behavior which resulted in the discharge of his firearm. As he headed toward home, he saw an apparition, or phantom type appearance in the likeness of little Bill King. Not understanding what he was seeing, he fired at it. The image appeared and reappeared several times. He said the last time he saw the unwelcome vision was when it disappeared in the spring from which the family carried their water.* It was clear Sam seemed to be shaken by the whole affair.

And now, as the great late Paul Harvey so often said, "the rest of the story." Sometime during the night Dan Long died, which was expected, with family members gathered near him. What was not expected, a few miles away along Silver Creek, someone found the body of Little Bill King. No, he had not been shot, but had fallen from his horse and died of natural causes. No one to my knowledge ever questioned the validity of Sam's experience. There were many in the house who heard the shots, and heard Sam's explanation. When word reached their ears about Little Bill, it no doubt gave them something to think about. I'm sure it would have made me pause and think.

* I have an old B&W photo of that spring taken in the summer of 1954.

Samuel "Sam" Long

The following will consist of some trivial as well as factual information relative to my great uncle, Jeff Long. Jeff is one of three older brothers of Sam Long, the subject of the preceding segment. My grandfather, Leslie A. Long being the eldest of eight children of Daniel and Laura Belle Hickam Long.

In the book, "The Hills that Beckon," this author was privileged to include some interesting information concerning Jeff, thanks to the input of various willing participants.

As a small child, I recall Jeff stopping by our house from time to time when my family lived on Moberly Branch, although I did not see him often. I always thought he had a striking resemblance to my grandfather, Les.

In the "Hills That Beckon" there were some subjects which I avoided for fear some family members might be offended. As long as I can remember there were certain members of my family who would comment on the way Jeff would use the word, "their," when referring to they, them or even the word it. An example: If the word usage was, "they had better be careful," Jeff would phrase it, "their had better be careful."

I was very sensitive about sharing Jeff's pet word until I met Jeff's son, Orbin at a family type reunion in the nineteen eighties and was surprised to find Jeff's own immediate family picked up on his word usage when quoting their father. I was relieved to know I would no longer have to be on guard to save feelings as the family thought it was humorous also.

From what I have learned about Jeff's skill in dealing with certain situations, such as horse and mule trading as well as other matters, he was not one to be outdone when it come to bargaining with an opponent. I have a feeling he was being ignorant, "like a fox" when he would tell someone a far fetched tale just to see how they would react.

A classic example of one of these declarations was in 1964 when he announced everyone should get a supply of beetle dust. He had just heard on the radio that America was going to be invaded by beetles. He did not mention the beetles were named John, Paul, George and Ringo. Another such announcement was made in July of 1969 when America made their heroic landing on the moon. It was clear that technology was allowing communication from moon to earth and Jeff concluded, at least to the casual observer, a long pipe was used to complete this activity.

Maybe he was serious, who knows? But then again, he may have been pulling the other party's leg. What I have learned about Jeff, he could very well have had the last laugh.

At a book signing in Richmond for "The Hills That Beckon" in either 2004 or 2005, Jeff's son-in-law, Glendon Dargavell shared the following story which attests to Jeff's keen appetite for the art of bargaining.

As the story goes, Jeff found a .22 caliber rifle submerged in a creek or small stream. He retrieved it from it from the murky depths and carried it home. He was not sure what he was going to do with it, from all appearances it was of little value. The mechanism, including the trigger and hammer, if it had one, was no doubt rusted solid.

By this time there were a few small Kentucky towns attempting to hang on to court day. However, the events had become nothing more than glorified flea markets. One of the most popular of these events was in the town of Mt. Sterling of which Jeff enjoyed attending. Jeff, his son Orbin, his son-in-law Glendon along with the prized firearm headed for Mt. Sterling. Jeff was determined if this item had any value at all, he was going to take advantage of it.

Probably to Jeff's surprise he did encounter an individual who expressed some interest in the forlorn item. The potential customer asked Jeff if the gun would snap, to which Jeff replied, "I'll guarantee you their won't snap."

Jeff's son, Orbin, recently confirmed witnessing this deliberation between his father and the possible buyer. Not sure if the transaction ended in a sale.

The following is a much needed correction of the list of Jeff's children as reported in "The Hills That Beckon." In the list previously reported, Alene was inadvertently listed as Jereal Dean. Also Oma and Alma were listed as dying at an early age. This is true relative to Oma, there was no Alma.

Thanks once again to Orbin Long, and his dear wife, Greabith, for coming to my aid in supplying a true and dependable listing of Orbin's brothers and sisters in chronological order.

Four children by Belle Smith

Laura Belle
Charles Daniel
Thomas
Dora Mae
The remainder by Stella Masters

Della
Oma Died, 3 wks. old
Russell Lee
Geneva
Fannie Moore
Orbin
Alene
Milton Way
Elsie
Opal
Thelma Marie Died, 4 yrs. old
Betty Lou and Morris, Morris died, 3 days old

Jeff Long and wife Stella

Orbin Long, Jeff's Son

Another entry from my grandmother's scrapbook

Growing up in the Poosey Ridge area, I knew Bill Cates by sight and reputation only. He seemed to be a man of varied interests and talents, farming and truck driving to name a few. The names of Bill and Goldie Cates were well-known to most Poosey residents. The following will depict an article in the Richmond Daily Register as closely as possible with two minor changes. The article reported he was the son of the late Mr. & Mrs. Charlie Agee, and she the daughter of Mr. & Mrs. George Cates, of which the opposite is true. It looks as if the celebration was on the actual anniversary date of September 2, 1978. The article reads as follows.

COTTONBURG COUPLE WED 70 YEARS

A Cottonburg couple reached a milestone in their lives Saturday, September 2 that very few people ever hope to achieve.

Mr. And Mrs. William Cates observed their seventieth wedding anniversary and were the incentives for a family luncheon on Sunday at their home.

Mr. Cates at the age of 18, was married to Goldie Agee, 14, on September 2, 1908 at the Madison County Courthouse. He was the son of the late Mr. & Mrs. George Cates and her parents were the late Mr. & Mrs. Charlie Agee all of Madison County.

Mr. Cates has been a farmer in the Cottonburg area where they have always made their home and they are affiliated with the Gilead Baptist Church.

They were the parents of seven children including Mrs. Ernest (Ethel) Collins, George B. Cates, Mrs. Clay (Carrie) McCulley, Mrs. Ed (Stella) Davis, Mrs. William Clay (Ann) Masters, Mrs. Carter (Mable) Prather, and one who died in infancy named Ina. They have 11 grandchildren, 17 great grandchildren, and 10 great great grandchildren.

Five generations are carrying the Cates name through the first son in each family.

Thirty-three members of their family gathered Sunday to pay them tribute on the occasion at the bountiful luncheon which was highlighted by the delicacies of the summer season. All their children and all of their grandchildren, with the exception of two, were present for the event and showered the couple with gifts. They were presented with a beautifully decorated cake bearing the inscription "Happy 70th anniversary Mom and Pop" which graced the table along with an arrangement of garden flowers.

Mr. and Mrs. Cates are in fairly good health, considering their age, and are able to care for themselves and maintain their own home.

Author's note: Received the sad information 3/17/09. Ethel Cates Collins,99, of Poosey Ridge, widow of Ernest Collins, passed away Saturday, March 14, 2009 in the Telford Terrace Nursing home.

A brother, George B. Cates and sisters, Carrie McCulley and Mable Prather had preceded her in death along with her parents.

The following is another bit of nostalgia offered by Neal B. Whittaker. Those of us who are familiar with the Poosey Ridge area are aware of the fact many folk were known by their nickname. There will be only a limited representation of all the names he was kind enough to share. The names will not be listed in any particular order.

NAME	NICKNAME
Jess Land	Crit
Coleman Baker	Bud
Harold Taylor	Babe
William Clay Masters	Duff
Vernon Clay Ham	Scrub
Harlan Reynolds	Cork
Virgil Land	Jack
Wilburn Land	Bib
Johnny Price Elswick	Preacher
Rufus Land	Tag
Phillip Roberts	Doc
J. W. Davis	Sha-bo
George Felix Teater	Pappy
Texie Ellen Teater	Mammy
James Middleton	Turkey
Delbert Howard	Deb
Thurston Click	Curt
John I. Sallee	Bud

| Wilbert Davis | Slow Boy |
| Sterling Moberly | Father Bear |

RECENT AREA CHURCH INFO

For the first recorded public religious service held in Kentucky, the "sanctuary" was the shade of a great elm tree; the preacher was the Rev. John Lythe, of the church of England; the congregation, a group of hardy settlers of the Transylvania Company ; the date, May 28,1775; and the place, Boonesborough, in what is now Madison Country.*

From its inception, churches and religious freedom have been a central component in the lives of the residents of Madison County. This is no less true today which is evidenced by the number of houses of worship continuing to increase across the landscape of the county.

In Forrest Calico's book, "A Story Of Four Churches", he focused on the following churches, Gilead, Salem, Friendship and Corinth. In the book, "The Hills That Beckon," this author covered Gilead, The Poosey Methodist Church and Salem Christian. Even though the coverage may be minimal on some subjects, there will be an attempt to feature a quantity of five houses of worship.

*Extracted from "Glimpses Of Historic Madison County by Johnathan T, and Maude W. Dorris.

FRIENDSHIP

From what can be pieced together relative to the history of this old church, it had a rather difficult time materializing. Constituted about 1883 and construction beginning some time afterwards, it was not until 1899 the church was dedicated.

In Forrest Calico's book, "A Story Of Four Churches," he states he was present for this event. He says there was a very large crowd in attendance with dinner on the grounds. He also goes on to say, John G. Pond was one of its first pastors. Calico's book was published in 1946, and at the time he commented, "I am informed that there is no longer any activity here, which is to be regretted."

Paraphrasing the first few lines from Calico's book, he says the church was located about one and one-half miles below the old stone house on Silver Creek near what used to be called Mose Stocker's spring and adjoining "The Maggie Smith Graveyard."

The church was located on the west side of Silver Creek and the old stone house he refers to is, or was, at the end of a road called Stone House Hill.

In the mid Nineteen Eighties this author had attempted to locate the old church building going down Stone House Hill from Poosey Ridge Road, but to no avail, since there was no access going north on the west side of Silver Creek.

Later, I was privileged to be introduced to a gentleman who was known by his friends and acquaintances as "Preacher Sallee," who was familiar with the area. If I ever knew his given name, it has been lost to my memory. He was kind enough to drive me down to Silver Creek from the east side from Newby. On the way down, he shared with me the sad news the old building had recently burned to the ground. We were in his pick-up truck and the creek was at a level where there was no problem to drive across to the location.

All that remained of what was once Friendship Church, were the flat stones used to form the foundation. They were still laying in the order in which the building was constructed.

Even though I was unable to view the actual building, I do have a photograph of the old church building which, I am sure, was taken many years after activity ceased. This photo was a gift courtesy of Mrs. Edith Kanatzar Stocker, who grew up in the Newby area. She shared with me after the church had discontinued regular weekly services, former members would have home comings from time to time and she and others would ride horseback from Newby, and across the creek to these events.

I cannot be sure as to what denomination Friendship associated it's self. Mrs. Stocker and me had a discussion concerning this matter. She was of the opinion it was a Christian Church, however, since John G. Pond, a dyed in the wool Baptist was pastor at one time, it gives cause to wonder.

Adjacent to the church property is the Friendship, or Maggie Smith graveyard. This country cemetery is very old and precedes the origin of the church by many years. There are several civil war veterans buried here. They are identified with 1st Ky cavalry etched on their markers, however most of them are not dated. An example of an old marker, Capt. Nelson Burrus, Co. K, 1st Ky Cav., Mexican War Veteran 1827-1908.

Some of the first families to become a part of the beginning of Friendship are familiar names to to this area. They were Sallee, Moberly, Reynolds and Chandler.

When Calico mentioned in his book, which was published in 1946, there was no longer any activity there, the church existed less than fifty years from the time of it's dedication in 1899.

From an early age growing up in the Poosey/Silver Creek area, I have heard many folk speak of Friendship Church, my own family included.

In the early nineteen eighties at one of the Gilead Baptist Church home comings, I heard Neal Prather, a local Baptist minister inquire about Friendship.

Even though the old church's history was short lived by standards set by other churches in the community, it still seemed to have an impact which existed beyond the building itself.

Friendship Church

CORINTH CHRISTIAN CHURCH
1100 BOGIE MILL ROAD

When "The Hills That Beckon" was written, the focus was primarily on Poosey Ridge and the west side of Silver Creek, therefore, Corinth was not included. This narrative, however, is not limited to any one area, as the title infers, "Beyond The Hills That Beckon."

I am certain there is little this author can share with the members of Corinth they do not already know, with able historians such as Alma Stone* in their midst. I feel sure most members are aware of the young Australian minister who when walking to preach at Corinth, encountered what he thought to be a chipmunk which turned out to be a skunk. Also, the account of Dr. Phillip Roberts, a charter member who was a lieutenant in The First Kentucky Cavalry, Company K, and made a heroic escape after being captured in Tennessee during the civil war. Forrest Calico went into detail on both of these episodes in his book, "A Story Of Four Churches."

Since Mr. Calico's book was published in 1946 with an excellent history of the church, this author will make an attempt to focus more on what is happening and what has happened in the life of Corinth in the twentieth and twenty first centuries.

*Before continuing, I would like to pay special acknowledgment to Alma Stone for supplying me with data and documentation on Corinth today as well as the not too distant past.

Most Christian Churches (Disciples Of Christ) in Madison County which were constituted prior to 1830 were in all probability Baptist churches. The reason for the change was due to the influence of Barton W, Stone, Thomas Campbell and his son, Alexander. It seems Stone and the Campbell's were laboring in the same vineyard, one not being aware of the other. While Stone had some doctrinal disputes among the Presbyterians, the Campbell's were having similar problems among the Baptists, their denomination of choice at the time. Alexander Campbell published a paper called the Christian Baptist while Stone's paper was called the Christian Messenger. Alexander Campbell and Barton Stone met for the first time in Georgetown, Ky in 1824. They became steadfast friends and were in complete sympathy, one with the other. In January, 1832, a meeting was convened in Lexington, Ky., with the view of uniting these two movements into a permanent union. From this time forward, especially in Madison County, the movement saw steady growth.

Corinth, however, has been a Christian Church from its inception as it was not organized until July, 1885.

The following is an attempt to draw back the curtain of time to an era when seeds were sown by a dear lady which ultimately blossomed into what is now Corinth Christian Church.

In the spring and summer of 1882, Sister Sallie Roberts succeeded in getting James Long and S. C. Bogie to help her start a little Sunday School on the branch, also known as Bogie Branch, at the Roberts school house. The Sunday School classes continued until 1884 when Owen Young held a series of meetings at the old Bogie Mill. Harrison Spainhower was running a distillery near the old mill and he had his whiskey barrels stored in the mill house. Bro. Young used three of the whiskey barrels for his pulpit during these meetings. Bro. Young was a county evangelist employed by the county cooperation and sent by them to hold the meetings.

The meetings were so successful that the people of the community contributed a few hundred dollars to build a church building. They appointed a committee to select a suitable site for the building and appointed D. T. Bogie Sr, Irvine Roberts, James M. Long and S. C. Bogie to serve on the building committee.

Dr. Philip Roberts donated an acre of land for the church building and in the spring of 1885, contractor William Barnes began erecting the building. It was completed in July of that year.

Corinth Christian Church was organized in July 1885 and on the second Sunday in May 1886, Bro. C. P. Williamson held the dedication service which was attended by a large crowd and included all day services and "dinner on the ground."

Charter members were:

D. T. Bogie Sr.	S. C. Bogie	Ella Cooley
Albert Long	James M. Long	James Merit Long
Dr. Philip Roberts	Clarkie Roberts	Irvine S. Roberts
Robert Roberts	Nannie Taylor	Linda S. Willis
Martha Bogie	D. T. Bogie Jr.	James Griggs
Martha Long	Amanda Jane Long	Laura Long
Nannie Roberts	Cassinda Roberts	Sallie Roberts
Pauline Roberts	John M. Willis	

There have been many ministers who have served the congregations of this church through the years. Those whose names have been recorded are:

Owen Young	Riddle	Lunsford
Neal	Lynx	D. G. Combs
Gadd	Morgan	J. W. Prather
W. I. Peel	Green Stocker	Milt King
Victor Lackey	Russell Dietch	Harold Newland

Willie Davis   Elmer Ray   Homer McNew
Noland Chandler   Ralph W. (Billy) Forquer

Noland Chandler served as pastor from 1951 until his death Dec. 1975. Ralph W. (Billy) Forquer became the pastor in Jan. 1976 after the death of Bro. Chandler. Bro. Forquer is the current pastor, as of this writing, and is now in his 33rd year of service at Corinth.

Author comments: Some of the foregoing names are familiar to the author, such as Green Stocker, Milt King, Harold Newland and Noland Chandler.

The name, Milt King has been familiar to the author his entire life, as has the name Noland Chandler. Like me, Rev. Chandler was a Poosey Ridge native whom I saw occasionally. I believe he worked at, what is now, Combs, Parsons & Collins Funeral Home in the early Nineteen Seventies. I saw him last at my grandfather's (Les Long) funeral in April, 1973.

Rev. Chandler died in December of 1975 after twenty four years of faithfully serving Corinth. He was replaced by Ralph W. (Billy) Forquer in January, 1976.

It is recorded that Rev. Owen Young, Rev. W. I. Peel and Rev. Green Stocker each preached six or more years at Corinth.

Milestones in the life of Corinth Christian Church

1951 – Corinth Christian Church held its first homecoming, and it has been an annual tradition since. Folks come from far and near each third Sunday in September to enjoy the day with friends and family.

1952 – Stained glass windows were installed in the church. Members (or families) contributed money to purchase a window, and donor names were inscribed on the windows.

1993 – The ladies of the church decided to make a cookbook. We searched for recipes from the families of many of those who had gone before us as well as our current congregation. The project was a great success with the sale of 600 cookbooks.

1998 – A fellowship room was added to the church which was a great upgrade to our building and provided an area for many activities, and potluck lunches.

1999 – A time long awaited for!!!!!!!! After our church had been in existence for 113 years we were finally getting access to a public water system on Bogie Mill Road. We immediately installed the water line to the church property.

2001 – We constructed another addition to the building which now houses a kitchen and two bathrooms. (The little house out back still stands in vine covered repose as a reminder of all the years gone by).

2005 – A permanent picnic shelter was constructed for outdoor activities. From 1951 until 1980, farm wagons were used as food tables at annual homecomings; after 1980 tents were rented and folding tables were used; with our new permanent shelter we no longer have need for the tents.

2005 – Handicap ramps and a concrete walkway was constructed from the back door at the kitchen around the church to the picnic shelter; Our handicapped friends can now access the entire building with out getting off the walkway.

2005 – Our flag pole was donated and installed by Doug Howard.

2008 – Corinth Christian Church purchased commemorative porcelain plates with a photo of the church on the front and a brief church history printed on the back. These plates are for sale to anyone who wishes to preserve a small piece of the history of this 124 year old church.

Once again Alma Stone will be referenced with, what is considered to be, or will be, as time unfolds, important Corinth history. In a recent correspondence she shared there is a lady, a Corinth member, who in her nineties sings a solo every Sunday, without music, and most of the time from memory. This dear lady is Hallie B. (Agee) Whitaker who has been a member of Corinth since the Nineteen Forties.

The following is an excerpt, and a direct quote from a message received from Alma in early 2009. It bears witness as to how important Alma and her late husband, Marvie, were to the life of Corinth.

"My husband, Marvie Stone Sr., passed away in 1995.He was Deacon, Sunday School teacher and Song Leader at Corinth for many years. He grew up in Corinth Church-the son of Price and Bessie Stone. Our pianist at Corinth passed away at age 83 (she played for the services on Sunday and died the following Wednesday). For quite some time we had no one to play the piano, so I decided since lots of people play the instrument it couldn't be that difficult to learn. I took some quick and condensed lessons from a local teacher who was willing to use our church hymn book as my textbook. She taught me enough to get me through several hymns and with practice I started playing for church at the age of 52 – I'm 68 now and they are still tolerating my attempt to play (or torture) the piano. I have also been Sec/Treas for Corinth since 1986. It seems I have the jobs no one else wants and every time I try to retire from them, no one will take them. Ha."

A fitting manner in which to end the segment on Corinth is to quote a comment made by Marvie Stone at the end of each service as he finished leading the congregational singing. He would always say to the congregation, "keep on keeping on, God will outlast the storm."

It seems the church body did in fact heed Marvie's sage advice as the church continues to flourish. These resilient Corinthians have outlasted many storms, and with their faith intact, will outlast many more.

Corinth Christian Church

Gilead Baptist Church
1279 Poosey Ridge Road
Richmond, Kentucky

The last time the author was privileged to attend Gilead was in September, 2006 as the old church was celebrating the 200th anniversary of being admitted to the Tates Creek Association of Baptists in 1806. There are church historians who feel Gilead was actually organized before 1806, possibly in 1796 or 97.

It was my good fortune to be able to attend the first Gilead Home Coming in 1982. The event was very well attended and the weather was perfect. As usual, the Gilead ladies did not spare the food, which was supplemented by other visitors.

Several years ago, in the rear of the church building a small basement was provided to be used for Sunday School classes as well as space for fellowship events. Some did in fact use this facility, especially in inclement weather. However, during the beginning of these events, large flat bed farm wagons were pulled into the front yard of the church. The wagons were used as tables to place the huge quantities of food which seemed to be adequate to fit the need.

As time unfolded and I was privileged to attend subsequent Home Comings, I noticed there were fewer familiar faces from year to year. The first Home Coming event I attended in 1982, I was re-united with long time Gilead supporters I had known since childhood. The following is but a partial list of the many friends, neighbors and relatives who were so familiar and important to me as a child.

The Taylor brothers, Frank, Darnell and Gordon, Lewis Ward, his wife Willie Moore and her brother, Lonnie Elswick. Duke Bellamy, Clyde Land, Roberta Long Evans, William D. Long, Betty Curtis, Stratton and Golda Stocker, Bud and Laura Edith Baker. As was indicated, the foregoing is but a partial list. However, as time progressed, the absence of these good folk became more and more conspicuous as one by one they were taken from us.

Another individual who seemed to never miss one of these celebrations is my aunt, Mary Laura Proctor. Mary Laura was born in 1917, and at this time in her life health issues prevent her from taking part in activities she enjoys so much.

There have been many physical changes in the building and grounds in the last several years. The first few years of my visits are marked with the memory of outdoor restroom facilities. As a child attending Gilead on a regular basis, I thought nothing of it. But in the company of my teenage daughter, it seemed a little strange.

But that was then and this is now. Gilead now boasts indoor plumbing and central air and heating. There has also been a shelter house constructed in back back of the property. During the period the present building was built,1892, it was common to have two front doors in order to gain entrance to the sanctuary. Gilead does in fact have two front doors and a section of steps for each door. Thankfully, for the physically impaired, a ramp has been constructed to gain entrance to one of the doors, because for some, the steps could be, and has been quite inconvenient.

In the long ago period the church was built, it seems two doors were necessary. At that time, the story goes, men and women entered separate doors and sat on separate sides of the sanctuary.

It would be safe to say, I am sure, the present building which was constructed in 1892 is the fourth building to house the Gilead congregation. Forrest Calico, in his book, "A Story Of Four Churches" writes, "No doubt the first building stood near the center of the old graveyard and near the road. It must have been of logs and used for preaching and teaching both." The old graveyard Calico refers to was at the extreme north end of the present cemetery. He also says preaching was done here near or after 1783. This is the reason this author believes Gilead had been in existence long before becoming a member of the Tates Creek Association in 1806. Calico goes on to say, "After a few years the old schoolhouse was torn down and rebuilt just opposite Aunt Fatima Tudor's where Mark Tudor recently lived in the lower corner of the present cemetery." This is not the same house but the same property where Lana Bellamy Vaughn now resides. The third house of worship to house the Gilead congregation was built in 1842 and endured until another, more suitable facility was built in around 1850 which endured until the present building was erected in 1892.

The building constructed in 1850 was located in the center of the present cemetery, where the flag pole now stands.

I think this old gentleman was mentioned in "The Hills That Beckon." I am referring to Morris Calico, a long time member of Gilead, and the uncle of Forrest Calico.

Uncle Morris, as he was called, was born in 1852. By the time I had become a regular attender of Gilead, he had removed to Garrard County and visited only occasionally. He seemed to get a kick out of talking to young people. It did not occur to me at the time, but later in life I could not believe I actually had a conversation with someone who could remember when Lincoln was shot. The conversations I had with him took place in the early Nineteen Forties when he was in his early Nineties.

Unlike today, my early memories of the Gilead Cemetery consisted of it being terribly overgrown. There was no scheduled plan to keep it mowed or the underbrush cleaned out. To put it mildly, most of the time it was in a terrible condition. Each time Uncle Morris would visit he would attempt to recruit workers to clean up the overgrown cemetery. As a rule he was pretty successful in his recruitment efforts which resulted in quite an army of volunteers. On the designated day, workers would show with scythes, weed blades, saws of different types, picks, axes and grubbing hoes.

A good days work would make a huge difference in the appearance of the old graveyard, but it never looked as good as it did in later years.

As I write this, I am reminded of a story my father used to tell. After one of Uncle Morris's pleas to clean up the cemetery, my father and another man were walking past the old graveyard when my Dad said, "well, it sure needs a good cleaning up." His companion replied, "It sure does, on judgment day, every body else will be half way to Lancaster before those people will be able to get out of there."

As was mentioned, my memories of the old graveyard consisted of it being overgrown and unkempt. All of this begin to change in the mid nineteen eighties, thanks to the efforts of Roberta Long Evans. Bert, as she was known by family and friends had attended Gilead as a child and young adult. Since moving to another section of the county, she no longer attended nor kept in contact with the old church. However, in the early nineteen eighties, especially when the homecoming events started, her interests were renewed.

After reuniting with the church, she, like Morris Calico before her, developed a passion to keep the cemetery more presentable to public view than was practiced in the past. Her efforts resulted in mobilizing crews for special work days on a regular basis. The workers came not only from the church, but from anyone she could recruit. Unsightly vegetation was removed, unwanted small trees cut down and the grass mowed. Grave markers which had fallen over were put back in place, sunken graves were filled in and re-seeded. As a lovely crocus emerges from the soil in the spring, so did the old cemetery begin to emerge as an image of a well kept country cemetery.

At this time in her life, Bert's health was beginning to fail, but she did not forsake her duty to the cemetery. Ruth Ross Mahanes, great grand daughter of John G. Pond, long time pastor of Gilead, remarked the first time she saw Bert, she was in the center of the cemetery on a walker. She went on to say she had to find out who that woman was.

We lost Bert December 27, 1992. However, a few years prior to that sad day, Gordon Taylor, who grew up not far from the old cemetery, saw the need to perpetuate it's care and maintenance well into the future. Gordon, who lived in Richmond and was involved in the Real Estate and Insurance business, had been working for some time with local attorney, Charles Coy to form an Interest Bearing Trust Fund. This trust would also include a board of directors.

Evidently the plan is working well as my last visit to the old graveyard saw it mowed and well trimmed.

A very significant and memorable day for the old graveyard was November 12,1989 when the first American flag was raised over Gilead Cemetery. The moving ceremony was conducted by DAV, Disabled American Veterans from Lancaster. An all weather flag was donated by Senator Larry Hopkins. The flag pole was donated by three of Colonel John G. Pond's great grand children. They are Lina Pond, Ruth Mahanes and M. K. Ross Jr. Colonel Pond is buried in Gilead cemetery, and it had always been a dream of the three to see an American flag flying over the cemetery.

It was mentioned earlier the role Roberta Evans had in cleaning up the cemetery. During the ceremony, she was presented a plaque of appreciation. As Earl "Doug" Howard raised the flag pole for Corinth Christian Church, he also raised the pole for Gilead. Frank Taylor was awarded the honor of custodian. This author can speak with some authority concerning many of the details surrounding this auspicious occasion since he was present at the event.

The flag pole is located in the center of the cemetery near where the 1850 building was located and remained until the present structure was built in 1892.

In the mid to late Nineteen Eighties, there was a collection of flat stones near this site and it was said they were the remains of the front steps of the 1850 church. I have a photo in my files of these stones photographed in the late nineteen eighties.

Gilead has been a part of the Poosey Ridge landscape for well over two hundred years. Some of my earliest memories go back to this old church. I believe I mentioned in the "Hills That Beckon," I can remember the kerosene lamps with their reflectors mounted on the walls, as well as the circle of lamps mounted in a wagon wheel type fixture suspended from the ceiling.

There are few today, especially current church members, who can recall when Poosey Ridge road was not paved, or when REA first introduced electricity to Poosey.

Gilead has been fortunate in the past several years to have had devoted pastors who were capable of developing and nurturing the Gilead flock into a stable fellowship.

In a recent phone conversation with Mrs. Frank "Irene" Taylor, she shared they are averaging around fifty for Sunday morning worship, and it seems most everyone is more than pleased with their new pastor, Mark Gabbard.

During one of the events held at Gilead in the late Nineteen Eighties, I was privileged to talk to a resident of Garrard County. He said as a child, his family considered Gilead to be the big church in the community. He went on to say, especially in the late afternoon, from his home on Jolly Ridge, when the bright sun shown toward Gilead, it showed up like a diamond from that distance. Since the construction of the current building in 1892, which was a rather large facility for the time, there have been many drawn, like the Jolly Ridge resident, to the Gilead Baptist Church.

THE SALEM CHRISTIAN CHURCH

Forrest Calico, in his book "A Story Of Four Churches" tells us Gilead was originally built in an area called "the wolf pen." In like manner, Salem was built in an area described as "bear wallow," which indicates the primitive nature of the type of terrain the two buildings were built. Calico also states up until around 1850 the church was known as "bear wallow" as often as it was called Salem. Also, like Gilead, there were probably at least three buildings which preceded the current structure which was built in 1952 and dedicated in June of 1953.

Salem was organized in 1808 and growth was steady. One of the early buildings was a log structure which endured until just prior to the civil war when it was destroyed by fire. The church body did not have access to a house of worship until two years after the war ended when a new building was constructed in 1867. This period was a trying time, especially in the eastern half of the United States. I can find nothing to support my theory, but I would speculate services were held in homes of the parishioners until a suitable house of worship was built. It is said when the old church was razed in 1952, the date, 1867 was found etched in one of the foundation stones.

Once again, Salem was without, what some I am sure, considered to be a designated house of worship. This was a very temporary inconvenience to say the least.

I am not sure of the date of the last worship service in the old building, but there had been preparation to continue services to be held elsewhere until the new edifice was completed.

The author was not aware of the temporary location where Salem met for worship until the last few years. However, he was very much familiar with the delegated choice of collective assembly, since he had visited this building many times when his family were residents of Dry Branch Road. The building chosen to house the worship services of Salem, while the new structure was in progress was the former store building operated by Mike Bogie at Bradshaw's Mill at the end of Dry Branch Road on Paint Lick Creek. This location is sometimes referred to as Bradshaw Mills. There was a milling company in operation here in the late Eighteen Hundreds and into the early Nineteen Hundreds. There were two millers who operated the mills, the first, a man named Potts and the second, Les Bradshaw. There were others who were millers prior to the two mentioned, however, the name of Ben Potts and Les Bradshaw were more familiar to members of my family.

The old store building which Salem chose as their temporary house of worship as the new edifice was under construction is still standing as a tribute to the various type of of service it has rendered through the years. Although physically ravaged by time and the elements, and in disrepair, the Salem folk have a link with this old building as it sets facing Paint Lick Creek watching the endless waters flow into the Kentucky River.

There have been many improvements since the new building was dedicated June 7, 1953, such as the addition of a baptistery installed in 1968. A new fellowship hall has been added as well as new pews.. I have been told of an old well in the front of the church which many considered a danger to small children. I understand that well has now been filled in and is no longer a threat.

This author has always been impressed with the care and attention given the Salem cemetery. Unlike many such congregations, the cemetery has become an important component in the life of the church as well as the building and grounds. Each year the church hosts an annual Salem Cemetery business meeting with lunch served in the fellowship hall. This author was privileged to attend such a meeting May 29, 2005. With organization of this type, it is easy to see why Salem boasts one of the most manicured and well kept cemeteries in the area.

This next segment may seem somewhat out of place in honoring Salem, therefore, I will ask my good friend, Doug Howard to share whatever burden he is called upon to bare.

In December 2008, I received from Doug via mail a most unusual gift, which at the time was not understood at all. It was a piece of finished wood, approximately 8 inches long x 1-1/2 inches wide x ¾ inch thick. At one end of the block of wood there had been expertly carved a shallow depression in order to accept a small piece of what I would consider to be Royal Blue glass. On the side of the wood block where the glass was embedded a white card was glued with the following words. "1952 Presidential Election, Salem Church, Poosey Ridge KY."

I immediately placed a phone call to Doug hoping for an explanation of this most unusual gift. I was successful in contacting Doug who shared the following story with me.

It seems within the pastoral and peaceful confines of a fellowship such as Salem, politics can be a fly in the ointment to some folk. This was especially true during the 1952 Presidential campaign between Adlai Stevenson, Democrat and Dwight David Eisenhower, Republican. Not only in the Poosey area, but all over the United States this was a fiercely contested campaign. As good natured as local or national politics will allow one to be during heated contests, the will to win still beats strong within the hearts of the supporters regardless of their political persuasion. According to Doug there was a few individuals who were very vocal in their support for Adlai Stevenson. There was a group who was just as adamant for Eisenhower who had secret plans they intended to employ in the event of a Republican victory.

As of November 1952 it seems contractor Burdette Land was making excellent progress in the construction of the new building, even the installation of stained glass windows, of which I am sure the parishioners were very proud.

As the results of the election unfolded, it did not take long to determine General Eisenhower was going to be a clear winner due to the television and radio coverage. The "I Like Ike" supporters hurried to put their celebration of victory plans into action. They supposedly placed a few sticks of dynamite, possibly too many sticks and possibly too close to the church, and when Stevenson conceded and the dynamite was ignited, some of the glass in the beautiful stained glass windows were shattered.

Doug shared sometime later he was doing some work around the church and begin to find the particles of Royal Blue glass on the ground. He collected some of the glass to preserve as part of church history.

Salem Christian Church

THE POOSEY COMMUNITY CHURCH
formerly Poosey Methodist Church

In a recent trip to the Poosey area, this author was surprised to see there was no longer a Poosey Methodist Church but in its place the Poosey Community Church. In the book, "The Hills That Beckon" there had been given considerable coverage to the development of the Methodist Church, beginning with the huge tent revival featuring evangelists E. T. Perkins and Roland Brooks. My family was living on Turner's Ridge at the time and we as well as others walked the entire distance practically every evening to attend these exciting services. They were indeed exciting for me as this was the first tent I was privileged to enter.

When this change was discovered, the sequel to the "Hills That Beckon" was already in progress. As had already been determined there was to be more attention given to churches in this volume than the former.

The author wishes to make it clear to the good folk of the Community Church he is not due, nor does he request a reason for the change. If the current members of the Poosey Community Church are happy with the present circumstance,that is all that really matters. It should be of no concern to anyone else.

In my last visit to the church, I took note of how well the property was cared for, with lawn mowed and trimmed with building maintained. I took the liberty of taking a photograph or two.

At the risk of clinging to the past, I have a distinct memory of the huge sign, or display in the front yard of the Methodist Church which depicted II Chronicles 7:14. I was always impressed by that display. In June, 1990 while working on "The Hills That Beckon," I arrived at the Methodist Church around noon on Sunday to find long time member, Obra Collins and pastor Ted Beam preparing to depart. I talked to them a few minutes and secured what information was available at the time. I then asked them to position themselves on each end of the display for a photograph. I am pleased to say I still have that photo in my file.

This author still holds dear the memories of the beginnings of the Poosey Methodist Church as I am sure future generations of The Poosey Community Church will do likewise.

The Poosey Community Church

AREA CLERGYMEN

THE REVEREND JOHN GRIFFIN POND
1812-------1898*

After more than one hundred years after his death, the name of John G. Pond is still familiar to some folk in the Poosey/Round Hill area. This author was personally acquainted with two of his great granddaughters and consider his great, great granddaughter, Jacquelyn Ross Golden a personal friend.

John's father, Griffin Pond came with the Craigs with what became known as the walking church in 1781 and organized the Gilbert's Creek Church in what is now Garrard County.

John married Selina Schooler in 1832. They moved to Round Hill prior to the Civil war. He served as pastor of various Baptist Churches during his ministry including the old Friendship Church late in his ministry. He was pastor of Gilead on numerous occasions in his long pastoral tenure. In Spencer's History of Kentucky Baptists, he quotes, "John G. Pond is one of the oldest and most prominent ministers of The Tates Creek Association, of which he has been moderator for some years past."

John G., who acquired the title of Colonel Pond, was instrumental in organizing Co. "A" of the 11TH Kentucky Cavalry from the Round Hill/Poosey Ridge area, which became known as Pond's Company. This area of Madison County was primarily pro- union. There are several grave markers in the Gilead Cemetery of Civil war veterans indicating they were members of Pond's Company.

It was mentioned the author was acquainted with two of the old Colonel's great granddaughters. They were Ruth Ross Mahanes of

Paint Lick, and Lina Pond. It is believed by some the name Lina, was taken from her great grandmother, Selina Schooler Pond. Lina was born in Round Hill and lived there until 1915 when her family moved to a farm in Deputy, Indiana. The author was privileged to visit her on at least two occasions thereby availing himself of some personal family information relative to the life of John G. It was obvious from her excitement in the telling of one story, John G's. Involvement in the Civil War battle of Perryville was one of her favorites.

On October 8, 1862, Confederate and Union military units collided near Perryville, Kentucky, in what would be the most ferocious battle fought in the campaign. John G., never one to avoid the call of duty was in the thick of this battle, according to family history. The sad word the family feared would come after hearing what a terrible battle occurred did in fact come. Much to the family's grief and horror, word was received John had been killed in action in one of the bloodiest battles ever fought on Kentucky soil. The family was making plans to go to Perryville and claim the body when much to their surprise and delight, John walked in the door.

There are some records which show John G. Pond dying in 1899.* However, his grave marker in the Gilead cemetery shows 1898, but after all these years what difference does one (1) year make?

In this author's personal opinion, the Round Hill/Poosey Ridge area should be honored to be able to claim a man of John G. Pond's stature as one of their own.

THE REVEREND MILT KING

Although not normally identified with the Poosey Ridge area, the name Milt King has been a familiar name to this author for a lifetime. I personally have heard nothing but positive comments concerning Reverend King. I'm sure I am the one who has been denied the honor, but I have never had the privilege of meeting the man. However, in the first grade at Kirksville there was a student named James King whom I was told was Milt's son.

When the plan was conceived to include Reverend King in this narrative, one of my family members in Madison County was contacted to see if any of his children were available to provide information, but was informed all of his children were deceased.

The following is presented from a combination of articles from "my Grandmother's scrapbook" as featured in The Richmond Daily Register. The articles will not be quoted as printed, but will be paraphrased from several different pieces of print media. As per usual, my grandmother did not date the printed articles. However, there are clues which help to zero in on approximate dates.

An excerpt from one of the newspaper clippings gives a mini-history of Reverend King's experience as preacher, pastor and church builder. The article goes on to say the Reverend King preached his first sermon at the Silver Creek School House located near Silver Creek on Lancaster Road in April, 1924. Since then, he has held revivals and preached in tents, homes, beneath shade trees and in churches throughout Madison and adjoining counties.

An almost sixty year old article which, fortunately has a date, reveals a yellow with age, practicably unreadable announcement accompanied by a photo showing a young Milt King wearing a dark suit, tie and hat, and holding a bible. The piece continues with, "On Sunday, September 3, 1950 the first service will be held in the newly constructed King's Tabernacle located on the Lancaster Pike, U. S. Highway 52 at Happy Landing. It was announced today that all denominations are invited to attend this opening service." (It is clear Rev. King welcomed other denominations since he was once pastor of Corinth Christian Church.)

The clipping proceeds by saying approximately five years ago the Rev. Milt King started holding services in a tent at Happy Landing. For five years the Rev. King and the citizens of this community have struggled to establish a church at Happy Landing. On September the 3rd this struggle will come to a successful conclusion. The citizens of this community have a new concrete and frame building in which to attend services, and will now be able to hold services the year around.

Another press clipping begins with the headline of "OPEN HOUSE TO HONOR REV. MILT KING SUNDAY," and announces an open house in honor of Reverend King, founder, builder and pastor of King's Tabernacle located at Happy Landing on Lancaster Road.

The reception will take place at the residence of his daughter, Mrs. Susie Frances King between the hours of 1 and 5 o'clock. The article goes on to say the celebration will take place Sunday, April 29th in observance of his forthcoming 88th birth anniversary on July 25th. (On this entry my grandmother had written the date, 1979.) The invitation continues by saying the Rev. King is the father of seven sons and three daughters who invite friends and relatives to attend.

The final presentation in this narrative shows a photo of an elderly couple with the following printed message. "REV. MILT KING REACHES AGE 89." The message beneath the photo reads; "The Rev. Milt King, pastor of King's Tabernacle at Happy Landing, is pictured with his wife, Lu Alta, on the occasion of his 89th birthday celebrated July 20 with a host of family and friends. After morning worship services at the tabernacle, the entire group proceeded to the Paint Lick Sportsman's club for a bountiful picnic lunch. Five generations of the King family were on hand along with his children, grandchildren, great grandchildren, brothers and sisters, to express congratulations. Entertainment was presented by the Happy Landing Gospel Hours Singers and the Rev. King was the recipient of a monetary gift on behalf of the parishioners in addition to other gifts."

The author wishes to thank The Richmond Register for allowing the use of some of their ancient articles published in The Richmond Daily Register. The author is also grateful his grandmother, Annie Long, who cared enough to preserve them during her lifetime.

Reverend Milt King

A Trip To The Holy Land

In July, 2008, in honor of my seventy fourth birthday, my daughter, Kathy, who is famous for giving me unusual gifts, outdone herself once again. After enjoying a birthday meal at her home, the time had come to open gifts. Her gift was a simple white envelope with a 3x5 hand crafted card inside. The card read,

CERTIFICATE
ALL EXPENSE
PAID TRIP TO
HOLY LAND (AKA KY)

This meant a trip to Poosey Ridge, she would be driving, I could go where I choose, when I choose and probably have lunch at the Cracker Barrel in Richmond.

On the chosen day, Kathy, her son, Matt and I departed Columbus, IN approximately 6:00 A. M. We picked up my son Tim in Louisville, who seemed to be always up for a trip to Poosey and sped off on I-64 E toward Lexington.

It normally takes three hours, more or less from Columbus to Richmond, and this trip was no different. We watched intently for the sign on I-75 which said "Eastern Kentucky University next right." We took that exit which led to Barnes Mill Road. Turning right on to Barnes Mill, we headed in the direction of northwest Madison County.

In keeping with the Holy Land theme which Kathy had coined, when we had reached our Jordan (Silver Creek) and unlike the ancient Israelites who forded the Jordan on dry land, we were allowed to cross it via a modern bridge. As we continued our pilgrimage, our next challenge was to scale the lofty heights of Mount Gilboa (Page Hill). The terrain seemed to level off considerably after Page Hill and after crossing the intersection of roads #876 and #595, it did not take long to arrive at what resembled a driveway to the right which led nowhere. This area has been undisturbed since the spring of 1974. This is the location of Whitaker's store 1904 -1974. Even though there were other owners involved, it was known as Whitaker's store from 1924 until 1974 when it was destroyed by a tornado. To some this austere parcel of land has become somewhat of a shrine, reluctant to see anything replace what was there.

Our first stop as we traveled north on Poosey Ridge Road was the Gilead Baptist cemetery. We inspected the graves of Daniel and Laura Belle Hickam Long, my great grand parents as well as the grave of a baby brother, Turley Moore Long, January 30, 1943- February 1, 1943. Since it was impossible to to take the old route down Moberly Branch due to the fact no vestige of a road was identifiable, we elected to choose Dry Branch as our next avenue of adventure. As we turned left off of Poosey Ridge Road into the entrance of Dry Branch Road, I was impressed in the manner in which Kathy's four wheel drive Subaru adhered to the steep incline.

As we gained the bottom of the hill and approached the first curve to the right, it seemed strange the home of Burdette and Marie Agee was no longer there. This white, well kept home seemed to be so much a part of the landscape of upper Dry Branch. As I surveyed the vacant area where the Agee house had been, I became painfully aware of my own failure to provide the information to round out the complete story of this good family. In "The Hills That Beckon," I referred to Burdette, Marie and their two children, Herndon and Barbara Ann. There was another, Ralph. The only excuse I have is the fact that both Herndon, whom we referred to as Royce and Barbara were near my age, whereas Ralph was born May 31, 1941. When my family moved to Dry Branch in the fall of 1942, he was only a little over a year old. Sad to say since he was not part of the gang, my memory failed to register him. Let me add, I'm sure this is but one of many errors to be found in the original text.

Ralph did in fact distinguish himself in various areas such as being a residential building contractor and a master carpenter. He was also an avid bass fisherman having competed in and won several tournaments.

We lost Ralph all too soon in March, 2006.

After descending to the bottom of the hill from Poosey Ridge Road, Dry Branch Road became quite level all the way to Paint Lick Creek. There were many curves, but no hills to deal with. After passing the Agee property, we continued on down the branch road. In a rather straight area of the road, before reaching the next home on the left, where the Garnett Howard and Elba Tackett family lived at one time, there was a very old house on the right, next to the road which had been vacant and abandoned for many years. My grandparents, Les and Annie Long, their two sons Jim and Vernon lived in this house in 1918. In fact, my great grandmother, Mary Hutchins Campbell died in this house the same year. In my lifetime I recall no one living there. The last few trips I have made to Dry Branch showed no evidence of a dwelling ever existing in that location. There is a rather humorous story connected with this property which has persisted in my family for years.

My father, Jim was six years old during this time and his brother, Vernon was only fifteen months his junior. Even at this very early age they had observed when men traded horses a different type of language was used to reinforce their point of view. On this particular occasion the boys decided to engage in playing horse trading including as many expletives as their young minds could conjure up. They chose a location determined to be far enough from the house where they would not be overheard, they thought. When their zeal and passion in the art of horse trading reached its peak, they could not hear their grandmother Campbell say to their mother, "Annie, do you hear those children cussing?" Being the parent of two small boys the age of Jim and Vernon, I'm sure their mother maintained a disciplinary device of correctiveness of some type. Armed with whatever rod of discipline she had, or collected on the way, she hurried to the location where the air was turning blue with her son's profanity. Although my father was only six years old at the time, he never forgot the dressing down he received at the hands of his mother, nor the reason he was subjected to the punishment. Knowing my grandmother as I do, when she was out of the sight of her mother and the boys, she probably had a good laugh herself at their expense.

Proceeding on around the curve to the right, we headed in the direction of the property which my father purchased in the fall of 1942. The house and barn and few outbuildings were on the left side of the road. Actually, on a narrow strip of land between the stream and road. The majority of the small farm consisted of a hillside across the road from the house and barn and ran parallel to the road for some distance. At the end of the property line near what was called the Marg Turner Branch, the ground leveled off rather nicely and it was here we had our garden.

Across the Marg Turner Branch from our garden spot was the home of Ollie and Ethel Casey and their son, Albert Clay. Clay was a few years my senior, but that did not prevent us from becoming fast friends. We saw quite a bit of each other during this time period as we swam in Dry Branch as well as exploring the surrounding hills. It seems strange to refer to him as Albert, since the entire time we were together on Dry Branch I knew him by no name other than Clay.

In April of 2005 I was shocked to learn of Clay's death. He was seventy four years old and he and his wife Jessie had been married for 56 years.

I probably saw Clay last in the mid to late nineteen forties, however, my memories are very clear in my mind and I cherish each remembrance of him as we cavorted and frolicked along Dry Branch.

From this point on, we traveled directly to Paint Lick Creek, This portion of Dry Branch Road being very familiar to me. From the Ollie Casey property, we were only a hop, skip and a jump from where my family lived. Saturday was the usual day of the week when country people went to town, in our case, Richmond. The entire length of time we lived on Dry Branch, my father did not own an automobile. Therefore, unless we were fortunate enough to travel with a neighbor, or ride in the bed of my grandfather's large flat bed 1936 Ford truck surrounded by stock racks, we stayed home.

The Saturdays we did not go to town, to ease the pain, I was usually given a dime to squander on a Payday candy bar and a Royal Crown Cola. They were five cents each at Mike Bogie's store at the end of Dry Branch on Paint Lick Creek.

I normally would walk by myself the distance. As a result, becoming very familiar with the houses which dotted the landscape as well as the many flat board wooden bridges, with no side rails, which crossed the many small tributaries which flowed into the branch from the various spring fed streams which issued out of the hills.

I was normally well equipped for the trip be it winter, spring, summer or fall. In the winter or rainy season, Dry Branch Road could be difficult for a pedestrian, as many puddles of water collected in the route. From late spring to early autumn, there was no problem as I normally went barefoot. For en climate weather, I had a pair of rubber boots which served me well.

As our quartet of casual observers continued our journey toward Paint Lick Creek, I felt it was my duty to point out as many landmarks as I could recall even though it had been sixty five years since I had lived in that area. In spite of the fact many familiar houses were gone, I tried to recall who lived where.

Not too far down the road from where the Casey residence and on the same side of the road lived the Robert Warmouth family. The Warmouth's son, James R., would join Clay and I occasionally in our search for excitement. This property was also the first farm my grandparents, Les and Annie Long purchased in 1920 after their marriage in 1911.

Whether the actual homes were still standing or not, I tried to identify the locations of the dwelling places of Paul Rhodus, Robert Masters as well as others who lived in the area.

As with most streams, the farther it flowed, the wider and deeper it became. Just before it emptied into Paint Lick Creek, Dry Branch Road made an sudden turn to the left running parallel with the creek. When I was fortunate enough to traverse this land, one had to wade the branch as water flowed across the road. In dry weather there was usually not too much water to contend with. But, Kathy's Subaru did not have to negotiate this inconvenience as a bridge had been built across the end of Dry Branch quite some time ago.

Before arriving at the old store building, we passed what was known as the Clay Simpson home on the left which was near the store building. I believe Mr. Simpson owned the store building and rented it to Mike Bogie at this time. There had been several people who had operated the store over the years, Mr. Simpson being one of them. In a recent phone conversation with Curtis Bogie, Mike Bogie's son, he shared some other merchants to run the store were Jesse and Taylor Bogie.

Curtis also shared their family decided to end their careers as storekeepers in the mid Nineteen Forties and moved to Back Creek in Garrard County, just across the creek, approximately, from where the store was located. They must have removed to Buckeye, also in Garrard County since in Nineteen Forty Seven or Forty Eight they moved to the College Hill area, back to Madison County.

We stopped at the old store building for a while which conjured up many memories for me. The building showed signs of neglect and disrepair with unsolicited trees, brush and weeds growing up around it. I'm sure it was in better condition when Salem used it as their alternative meeting place when the new church was under construction. Gone was the long hitching rail which was located north of the front porch. I am assuming it was north, if in fact Paint Lick Creek flows from north to south. I can recall on a Saturday afternoon when there were many horses tied to that very useful and necessary, but rustic piece of equipment. Paint Lick Creek is the border separating Madison and Garrard counties. At that time there was no bridge connecting the two counties in this area. There were many folk who lived on the west side of the creek in Garrard who traded at the store. Those who wished to cross the creek either had to wade, drive their autos, if the creek was not up, or by horseback. At this time, for many, it was much easier to shop via horseback, hence, the many horses hitched to the rail on Saturday afternoon.

The road, which is still called Dry Branch Road runs parallel to the creek until it ends at what was once considered a ford where the creek was crossed by driving, wading or riding horseback across the creek. In August of 1998 I took a similar trip into this area and was forced to turn my 1996 Olds Cutlass around in the middle of Paint Lick Creek. However, much to my delight, and I'm sure to Kathy's, since she was driving, there had been a bridge built connecting Madison and Garrard Counties.

After locating a suitable place to turn the vehicle around, the four adventurers made their way back to Poosey Ridge Road and north toward the river. We headed for what I thought at the time to be The Poosey Methodist Church, but found it to be the Poosey Community Church. After a couple of photos of the church, we proceeded on to the Salem Christian Church. The book, "The Hills That Beckon" contained only a picture of the 1867 church, consequently, I was determined to photograph the present church building along with the new fellowship hall.

We limited ourselves to the parking area across the road in front of the church. We exited the car for a while to stretch our legs after our long drive. Tim and Kathy walked a short distance to where they could get a better look at the green rolling hills cascading one after another in the direction of Paint Lick Creek. After being enchanted, for a moment, by the natural beauty of the landscape, I heard Tim say to Kathy, "you know, I could live here." To which Kathy replied, "I could live here too." It must be in the genes.

After we felt adequate photos had been taken, we made our way back south on the Poosey Ridge Road.

Our next scheduled stop was the old Kirksville School, now the Kirksville Community Center since the new Kirksville Elementary School had been built and had been used for some time. A few photos were taken of the old building where my educational process began in 1940.

While we were there, we contacted two of my cousins, Orline Proctor Hensley and Frances Long Sexton via cell phone and asked them to meet us at the Cracker Barrel Restaurant in Richmond for lunch. We had already made tentative plans with the two cousins for lunch and the phone call solidified the appointment.

Orline is the daughter of my aunt, Mary Laura Long Proctor, and we would not think of being that close and not make an attempt to see her. I believe it was the year, 1947, when she and her husband, Luther, along with their two children Vernon J. and Orline left the Poosey Ridge area and decided to move near the Speedwell area. Luther purchased a farm which became their home for the remainder of their lives. Mary Laura still maintains her home there at the age of Ninety Two as of this writing.

After a pleasant visit with Mary Laura, it was time for the weary travelers to begin their long trek north.

I had noticed during other visits, Kathy and Vernon J., or Jay, as he was known by the family seemed to have no problem engaging in conversation. Kathy had noticed Jay preferred an arm's length relationship, demonstrating little affection for even a second cousin such as she. As we began to make our departure, Jay and another individual was working on a tractor near an outbuilding. Kathy walked boldly up to Jay and announced she was going to give him a hug. Jay attempted to avoid her advances by saying he was too dirty and greasy from working on the tractor. Not to be outdone, Kathy grabbed him and kissed him on the cheek. I think inwardly, Jay was pleased with this surprise attack since he was smiling broadly as we drove away.

POOSEY RIDGE

How would one describe it? The word, "bucolic" comes to mind, an early 16th century Latin term which is defined as relating to the characteristic of the countryside or country life.

Also, the word, "pastoral," which presents an idealized image of rural life and nature. The author must confess to being guilty of this one.

And of course the very familiar term, "agriculture," farming; the occupation, business, or science of cultivating the land, producing crops or raising livestock.

It is clear, all of the above is descriptive of the subject in question, even so, there is much, much more which can be said of the area which for so long has been known as Poosey.

There has been much speculation as to how the name Poosey emerged. There have been stories it came from a family named Posey who lived in the area. Also, according to Calico, possibly from a tribe of Poos Indians. I have never heard of anyone named Posey living in that area. The possibility of the name coming from Native Americans would have its beginning in an early pioneer time period. The author has in his possession a copy of a deed dated May 10, 1877 where Allen and Josephine Taylor deeded to the trustees of the Gilead Baptist Church one acre of land. The deed says nothing about Poosey Ridge Road, but says the property is located on the Goggins Ferry Road, which leads to the Kentucky River.

I have no knowledge if this situation still exists, but at one time it was common to refer to upper and lower Poosey. Forrest Calico, in his book, "A Story Of Four Churches" tells an amusing account of a lady who lived in the lower end of Poosey. She was visiting the

Gilead Baptist Church which was located in what was considered to be upper Poosey. After services, a gentleman, who was acquainted with her and wished to make her feel welcome asked, "how are things in the lower end?"

When the book, "The Hills That Beckon" was published in August of 2003, I was amazed at how many requests I received mainly because the book featured considerable coverage of Poosey Ridge. I have actually lost count of all the notes and letters informing me the writers roots began in Poosey. Even though many folk reside in other states, when they read or hear the name Poosey Ridge, they suddenly become very alert and wish to acquire more information.

The topography or configuration of the land it's self may be a surprise to some visitors. The hills are not high, but very, very steep. Poosey Ridge Road is a backbone type ridge lying between Silver and Paint Lick Creeks all the way to the Kentucky River. The following account attests to the steepness or incline of the Poosey hills.

In the mid 1930's my maternal grandparents, Denny and Fannie Anglin, along with two of their children, Ruth and Clifford, lived on what is now road #876 going toward Page Hill. They lived in the same house that Bud and Laura Edith Davis Baker lived in so long. When one walks across the road in front of the house, the person is confronted by a very steep hill which descends into a hollow. At this particular time, country stores received their soda crackers in a galvanized can, complete with lid. Similar to our 30 gallon garbage cans today, but not quite as large. Some people called them cracker cans while others referred to them as cracker barrels. These cans were very much in demand by customers of the country stores as they were ideal for storing different types of feed as well as for other uses. I don't know if merchants gave them to select customers or sold them. In any event, the Anglin family had at least one of these useful items. Ruth was born in October of 1920 while Clifford was born in July of 1925. The two, no doubt, were looking for something to entertain themselves when one of them came up with the idea of one getting into the can while the other rolled his or her companion down the hill, which resembled a cliff. In any case, Clifford came out the loser as he was destined to get into the can for probably the wildest ride he had ever experienced. He somehow survived, but as long as he and Ruth lived, they never forgot that experience. I have heard them tell the tale time and again. I don't know if there was a fence between the hill and the road or not. I doubt that any self respecting horse or cow would want to attempt climbing that steep incline in the pursuit of freedom.

There has been some controversy as to where Poosey Ridge actually begins. In my personal opinion, I always felt it began where roads #876 and #595 converge. However, I could be wrong, as there are some ancient maps which mention Poosey as beginning further north on the ridge road. I was interested in knowing how far it was from the afore mentioned roads, #876 and #595 to the Kentucky river. My good friend, Doug Howard, was kind enough to drive his truck to where the two roads converge and check the mileage all the way to the river. I was surprised when Doug reported the distance was 8.7 miles. I did not think it was that far. I have already thanked Doug privately and now I thank him publicly for his assistance.

When someone my age thinks back to the location in which he or she grew up, it is common to think of it in idyllic terms, rather than how conditions actually were. When my thoughts return to this period, I must confess, I see mostly sunshine, very little shadow.

Speaking of sunshine and shadow, I am reminded how I used to marvel at how these two phenomenons interacted with each other. When my family lived on what was referred to as Turner's Ridge, there was no point higher in the neighborhood. Even though it could not be seen, because of the trees from my vantage point, I was actually looking across Dry Branch Road to another hillside. On certain days when there were scattered clouds as well as considerable sun, I could stand for some time and watch the shadow of a cloud racing down one hill which seemed to be chased by the sunlight, and up to the top of the hill where I was standing. My apologies if my description is lacking to where the reader cannot share my fascination with this natural celestial demonstration.

Another natural occurrence which I became accustomed to seeing, but thought nothing about it at the time, was star studded nights. Living in an elevated geographical area such as Turner's Ridge on a clear, moonless night, there was no other light to distract from the starlit spectacle save the weak glow from various kerosene lamps from a window here and there. After I moved into an urban area where the stars had to compete with all manner of lights such as street lights, automobile headlights as well as many other types of illumination, the stars were no longer as brilliant. It is a sad indictment to have to admit, but there are times I find myself looking for a spot where I can check to see if the stars are still there.

Most of us are no doubt familiar with the term, "babbling brook". Another favorite past time of mine, especially when I was a resident of Moberly Branch was listening to the gurgle, or babble of a spring fed stream flowing out of one of the hillsides which flowed into Moberly Branch, which in turn flowed into Silver Creek. It is certainly difficult to describe, but there was something tranquil and serene about the melodic sound of the clear spring water as it lazily babbled along on its way to an unknown destination.

A dramatic change in the Poosey area compared to when I was a resident, is what most farmers thought to be eternal; tobacco. This was the "king" crop. There were those who thought it would always be the principle crop and would never entertain the thought of it being replaced. Nevertheless, with tobacco falling out of favor with many in the general public, farmers were forced to look for alternative crops.

There are many old landmarks which have disappeared from the Poosey scene, such as store buildings, the scales, which were a little north of Whitaker's store next to the road. These were heavy duty scales for weighing livestock etc. It was mentioned in the Tudor family sketch where John Tudor bought land across Poosey Ridge Road from the present Gilead Cemetery in 1818. If the house which became known as the John Tudor house was not there when he purchased the property, it appeared soon afterward. That old structure remained until the early to mid 1980S when it was razed. Many of the old homes which were familiar to so many have vanished from the landscape. Not only has this left a vacancy in the memory, but also in the consciousness of those who recall how things were, and will probably never be again.

Up to this point the emphasis has been mainly on the physical characteristics of the area. Although these attributes are indeed important and whether a community fails or succeeds lies with the people, always the people.

In 1996, Hillary Rodham Clinton published a book based on her speech, and the ancient African proverb, "It Takes A Village To Raise A Child." I never gave it much thought at the time, but looking back I cannot disagree completely with Mrs. Clinton's concept. One could not consider the Poosey Ridge area a village, but with its many ridges, hollows and branch roads which is home to many people, no one would disagree Poosey Ridge is a very rural area; but it is certainly not isolated. I may be wrong in my assumption, but I can think of no area along the ridge road where one would be out of the sight of a neighboring house.

This author was pleased to learn first hand how the residents of Poosey Ridge was quick to lend their care to their neighbor's children. In today's society parents are cautioned to keep a watchful eye on their children. I do not recall this type of fear ever pervading the thought process where child care was concerned. As a youngster, this author felt free to go wherever he wished, as did others of the same age group, without fear of any type of confrontation. If we had to be cautious at all, it was in passing someone's home where an over protective dog wanted to prove he was in charge of security of that abode. If the animal exhibited behavior considered to be too aggressive, someone in the house would appear at the door and command the dog to cease and desist. If vocal commands were not effective, a few well placed blows with a tobacco stick were implemented. If these measures were not effective, stones, which were easily found were used to send the offender scurrying to a sanctuary of safety.

There were ancient trails or paths which by the early nineteen forties, the property they crossed had been fenced either with woven wire or rock fences. The rock fences had been erected long before woven wire had been developed. Most everyone in the area knew where these old familiar paths were, including the children. The property owners were well aware of these ancient routes and had no objection to them still being used. However, there was danger to be considered in these fields which surpassed the fear of dogs. Many farmers who raised cattle would also have a bull or two as part of his herd. It seems every young boy or girl who traversed these old trails knew where the bulls were and made every effort to avoid them. I must admit I have never been chased by a bull, but I have been chased by a cow which was protecting her calf that was only a few days old. There was no threat to the calf, but the cow surmised I was getting too close.

Apart from the above mentioned dangers, the Poosey Ridge youth seemed to have nothing to fear. If a misdirected young person found him or herself in an area where they did not belong, the good folk of Poosey Ridge would come to their aid, at least they did in my case and others whom I knew. If some adventurous lad had expectations of going swimming in a farm pond the owner considered to be too deep for safety, the farmer would not allow the boy the privilege. Again, I reiterate, the Poosey Ridge area residents felt it their duty to care for their neighbor's children.

Unlike many areas today, parents did not have to be concerned about their children falling into the hands of child molesters or offenders. The author does not wish to apply children were free to travel at will wherever and whenever they wished. When a child wanted to visit someone, they had better get their parent's permission and a time limit as to the length of time they would be gone. Not playing by the rules was a sure way of not getting to repeat the enjoyable experience.

Does anyone ever talk about, or even remember the big marble ring, or Stand Around (the old Wylie school), both located on the New Road?

I used to think it was something when I encountered someone who could recall when Poosey Ridge Road was not paved. Now, in my twilight years, I can recall when Turner's Ridge Road and Dry Branch Road were not paved. A good portion of Barnes Mill Road was paved in the mid to late Nineteen Twenties. My great grand father, William J. Campbell, who died in 1929, referred to the portion which was paved as "the slick pike."

The foregoing subject matter relative to Poosey Ridge is this author's feeble attempt to bathe the memory of his former dwelling place in a golden light of memory. Looking back, the sky seemed a little bluer, the sun a little brighter, the grass on the steep hills a little greener and the water in the streams a little clearer. I'm sure many of the residents of the same area during the same period would not experience the same enraptured impression as has been affirmed thus far.

No doubt the passage of time has aided this writer in fantasizing the splendor of the hills, hollows and the general local which has contributed to the thought process in describing Poosey Ridge. However, this author is more than pleased to say he is not alone in his admiration of the area. I am pleased to report there are many who are members of a mutual Poosey Ridge admiration society. Who knows, this title could generate a new organization. There are several former Poosey residents I have talked to who no longer live in the Poosey area, but whose roots are firmly embedded there, or even if they have never lived there, but their ancestors did, they still are proud to lay claim to their connection with Poosey Ridge.

KIRKSVILLE SCHOOL

My brief tenure at Kirksville School began in September of 1940. How vastly different was this experience, especially to a farm lad whose early years were spent on Turner's Ridge and Moberly Branch. Along with several other Turner Ridge kids, we made our way out the dusty ridge road to Poosey Ridge Road to ride the big yellow school bus driven by E. P. "Eph" Croucher.

I was not the only neophyte walking out the ridge feeling like a condemned criminal plodding down a long corridor toward his fate. As I recall, Charles Dalton's son, Lois was a first year beginner who was probably as uneasy as me. It was little comfort to us to have veterans, like Mildred Ross and Cecil Prather as companions. To complete this memorable day, my mother had dressed me "fit to kill," no pun intended. It was not unusual at that time for a boy to wear his best on the first day of school. The girls seemed to wear their best every day. But after the first week, many of the boys, including me, resorted to bib overalls. Now, back to the first day. I was the proud owner of a navy blue suit complete with jacket, short pants, white shirt, red tie white knee socks and white shoes. This dazzling wardrobe was topped off with a gray felt hat.

I was ushered into the first grade class of Mrs. Dovie Dudderar, a very pleasing lady. It seemed to be the custom, whether a lady was married or not, she was referred to as Miss. It was many years later I learned how to spell her last name and learned her first name was Dovie. Mrs. Dudderar had a son who also attended Kirksville. I do not remember his first name, but I do remember he wore knickers, or knickerbockers. I recall on one occasion he and another youngster became involved in an altercation. Mrs. Dudderar was made aware of it and brought the incident to an abrupt end in no uncertain terms.

Many of the students I already knew including William Leslie "Shorty" Davis and Lois Dalton. I became acquainted with Bobby Don Hale, Bert Ray Turpin as well as others. Sadly, it has come to my attention of the recent deaths of Leslie Davis and Bobby Don Hale.

I think it was the lunch break recess we were allowed to go out to the playground. I was still dressed in my suit, complete with hat. There was a short flight of stairs leading from the ground level to the first floor with a straight railing on each side. When the students entered the building at the end of the recess period, there was a mass of young humanity going up the stairs. Being the young gentleman I perceived myself to be, I removed my hat when I entered the building. I found myself on the extreme left of the crowd going up the stairs. Unfortunately, the end of the railing caught my hat and I was unable to dislodge it because of the multitude pressing forward. I was in a dilemma, I would not let go of the hat and the throng would not let up. Thankfully, I was rescued by an older student, I believe her name was Helen Cates.

As time marched on, the first grade begin to settle into a routine. At the end of the day Mrs. Dudderar would have the students line up at the classroom door in the order of their bus departure. Bert Ray Turpin, who was a tall, slender individual with blond curly hair, was waiting in line with his hat held with the inside of the brim next to the lapel of his coat when Mrs. Dudderar commented, "Bert Ray is holding his hat nicely." I tried to duplicate Bert Ray's posture with my hat, but alas, to no avail. I never received the accolades from Mrs. Dudderar she lavished on Bert Ray.

I soon become aware of other teachers who would have an impact on my early learning advancement. There was Miss Betty Curtis, Mrs. Lou Bach and Mrs. Lucille Whitaker. At the time, I thought Miss Lou's last name was pronounced, Back. Only recently have I learned her name was Bach, as in Johann Sebastian. I had known Mrs. Whitaker since early childhood. Early on in this narrative there is more definitive coverage given to Lucille and her two sisters, Elma and Ethel Turner, who were also teachers at Kirksville. Elma's last name was still Turner as of October, 1937 when the new High School was dedicated.

Other names which became familiar was Principal, Carl McCray, custodian, Lafe Duerson and bus drivers, E. P. Croucher, Ben Campbell and Dave Tussey.

I don't believe the boy's restroom, which was located on the second floor, had been completed by September, 1940. I recall attending an outdoor facility in back of the school building for a short time. However, it obviously did not take long to finish it because I did not have to follow that path very long.

I have tried to refrain from duplicating what was written in "The Hills That Beckon," however, I must reiterate the impact December 7, 1941 had on Kirksville School, Kentucky, and the United States as well as the rest of the world. I still feel a sense of pride in the way the Kirksville kids responded to the call to arms by participating in the scrap iron drives which culminated in a mountain of scrap iron on the front lawn of the school.

The following is a brief history of the old school. A special thank you is due Jacquelyn Ross Golden, a member of the last graduating class of Kirksville High School in 1955. Jackie was kind enough to provide documented data relative to the school's history.

Behind The Kirksville Baptist Church, there was a one room school used until a new building was built in 1912. There were eight grades, one teacher and room to accommodate up to ninety children. The new building erected in 1912 consisted of five rooms and five teachers. This building was in the vicinity where the 1937 building is located. Unlike the original school, there were twelve grades, non-accredited. In 1925 there were two additional rooms added along with two new teachers and the school was accredited as class B. Probably in 1936 or before. There was a decision by the school board to build another, more ambitious school complex. This new facility was dedicated October 24, 1937. The new Kirksville High School boasted an auditorium which seated up to 900, along with 21 rooms, 14 teachers, 12 grades and 413 children. An approved Class A school designed to meet the needs of rural people and the college entrance requirements for those who desired professional training.

The following will present the program for the dedication on Sunday afternoon at 2:00 o'clock, October 24,1937. However, before the presentation, I urge the readers of this book to reflect upon the word content found in this 1937 public school event compared to how it would probably be presented today.

PROGRAM

Prelude.....Faith Of Our Fathers...Mrs. Bach
Music...Rhythm Band, Harold Deatherage, Director
America The beautiful and There Is Music In The Air...... K. H. S. Glee Club
Dedicatory Prayer..Rev. W. P. Rogers Jr.
Address......... Superintendent of Public Instruction Harry W. Peters
Vocal Solo.............................. .... Thomas Bonny
Address...Lieut. Governor Keen Johnson
In The Garden ....Grace King, Francis Botkin, Betty Lock, Jennie Rogers
The Then And Now.. Milton Elliott
Acceptance Of The Building............................. Supt. J. D. Hamilton
The Dedication........................ S. E. Wheeler,Response by Audience

To the worship of God,
WE DEDICATE THIS BUILDING.

To the end that within these walls we happily may find him whom
to know aright is life eternal,
WE DEDICATE THIS BUILDING.

To the service of our nation, to the glory of our commonwealth, to
the enrichment of our smallest government unit,
WE DEDICATE THIS BUILDING.

In the hope that men and women assembled here may depart with the high ideal of patriotism, with the great desire for service, and with the ambition to be useful citizens,
WE DEDICATE THIS BUILDING.

To the amelioration of all classes, to the improvement of all professions, but more especially to that of teaching and learning,
WE DEDICATE THIS BUILDING.

Believing as we do that ignorance is the great curse of mankind, that without learning there is no vision and that without vision the people perish,
WE DEDICATE THIS BUILDING.

To the contemplation of beauty, to the understanding of music, to the inspiration of oratory,
WE DEDICATE THIS BUILDING.

To community life, to high school comradeship, and to the spirit of friendliness,
WE DEDICATE THIS BUILDING.

To the youth of our commonwealth who hunger and thirst for knowledge, who seek to attain scholarship that they may realize the joys that enlightenment brings as well as the opportunities for a life of greater usefulness,
WE DEDICATE THIS BUILDING

To the memory of those who have put their lives into this institution, whose very life blood has been poured into the building of this structure, whose spirit emanates from its every recess,
WE DEDICATE THIS BUILDING.

Likewise to the service of those yet among us, and of those who come after whose lives will be molded in similar patterns of unselfish altruism,

WE DEDICATE THIS BUILDING.

Finally, to whatsoever things are true, to whatsoever things are just, to whatsoever things are pure, to whatsoever things are lovely, and to whatsoever things are of good report,
WE DEDICATE THIS BUILDING.

Community Singing.. Mr. Bonny, Leader
Benediction.. Price Christian

One of the members of the 1938 Kirksville graduating class was Neal B. Whittaker who will be eighty nine years old as of July 25, 2009. Neal is very clear of mind at this point in his life and shared with me a few details of his experiences while attending Kirksville. He rode the school bus for most of his educational pursuit. He says Mr. Ben Campbell was the driver. He also says compared to today's luxury conveyances, with their comfortable padded seats and air conditioning, etc, his bus left much to be desired. There were wooden benches to sit on, and the windows were open, no glass. There were, however, curtains which could be tied back, if it was not too cold, or raining.

Some of the teachers he recalls during this period are, Mary Ellen Broadus, Madaline Roberts (Frazier) Whitaker and Verna Dunbar.

Principals who served at the new Kirksville High School were as follows,

1936-1938...............S. E. Wheeler
1938-1939...............Price Christian
1939-1955...............Carl McCray

In the very early nineteen forties, my family lived on Turner's Ridge. A short distance down the hill on Dry Branch lived Garnett and Dorothy Howard, and their two sons Gene and Earl Douglas, commonly known as Doug. I was able to be with the Howard boys for a short time before both of our families moved to other locations. In recent years, fortunate for me, I have been able to re-establish a friendship with Doug. We communicate by letter and by phone often. In June of 2008, it was my good fortune to be able to tour the Poosey Ridge area with Doug and a new found friend, Delroy Hisle. After a nice lunch at the Acres Of land Restaurant* at the top of Page Hill, we embarked on our adventure.

* I was horrified to learn this beautiful restaurant had been destroyed by fire in early 2009.

Doug was a member of the last graduating class of Kirksville High School in 1955. In May of 2005 at the fiftieth class reunion, which was conducted in the old building which had been converted into The Kirksville Community Center, Doug read a poem he had composed for this special event. This composition is presented in it's entirety from a manuscript given to the author by Doug.

THE CLASS OF 55

It was May of fifty-five
When we began to strive
To cure this world's ills
From the old Kentucky hills

Some went east
And some went west
Believe you me
We were some of the best

Some worked in factories
Some became a teacher
At least one of our group
Married a preacher

She helped him in his work
As they spread the word
Of the death on the cross
For this world's loss

Those that became a teacher
Helped make it a better world
As they taught and encouraged
Each boy and girl

For those that worked in factories
A good product was made
They followed the example
That others had laid

There are probably other careers
That I don't know
But I'm sure
They made a good show

In the cafeteria of old Kirksville
We had Beulah, Geneva, Lizzie and Dutch*
They cooked real good food
And fed us very much

Our principal was
Mr. McCray
He kept us straight
Day by day

Our janitor was
Mr. Nath Long
He'd tell us a joke
And sing us a song

Our coaches were
Hendren, Hammons and Wren
They were the best
There ever has been

Now Mrs. Curtis thought

I'd never be a poet
I guess she is right
And now we all know it

Now it's fifty years later
We stumble along the way
We drink prune juice
And use Ben Gay

As I look out I see
Senior citizens galore
With lots of grandkids
And hoping for more

The class of fifty-five
sure were lucky
We got our start
In old Kentucky

Doug Howard
May 2005

• Dutch, was Doug's mother, Dorothy Whitaker Howard.

Kirksville School

THE RURAL DEMONSTRATION SCHOOL

When my father finally decided he was through with farming, he sold the small farm on Dry branch and moved to another part of the county. By his own admission, he did not feel it was intended he should be a farmer. I have heard him admit to family members, who themselves were engaged in farming, "I can't even tell when my corn needs plowing." We left Dry Branch and the Poosey Ridge area, even though the hill's continued to beckon, and moved to Lancaster Pike, approximately two or three miles west of Richmond's city limits. He asked for, and was given a position with the Madison County Road Department and worked until he gained employment with the Kentucky State Highway Department. He seemed to find his niche in this type of work, and due to the fact we moved to a location which boasted twenty five acres, we still had the allusion of country living.

Up to this time I had attended Kirksville School, a rather large facility with grades one through twelve and a separate room for each class. There was also a full size gymnasium, cafeteria and indoor plumbing. The Ted McElroy family were our neighbors, and I discovered their son, Ollie Joe, attended the local school which I was destined to attend. Ollie Joe, who I recall was a year or two older than me, was a very friendly individual and eager to aid this emigrant from Poosey Ridge, and help him discover just what it meant to change schools for the first time.

We rode the school bus the short distance to the school, and as the big yellow conveyance careened up the narrow driveway, what a surprise it was to find this relatively small brick structure, grades one through eight in the same room, no cafeteria, no gymnasium and outdoor restroom facilities. I soon learned the name of the school was The Rural Demonstration, which was, by arrangement with the county department of education, operated by Eastern State Teacher's College, now Eastern Kentucky University. It was constructed as Eastern's model one-teacher school and located on the college farm adjoining the campus. The school had a ready supply of teachers, as this model school was a training ground for young would-be teachers entering into that profession.

The western part of the Eastern campus could be seen clearly from the school property. No doubt when the brick structure was constructed, it was on a knoll facing Kentucky state highway # 52, but when the new road was planned every attempt was made to eliminate every hill possible. As a result of the development of the new road, a mini canyon was cut through the hill in front of the school property leaving the school practicably isolated from view. In fact, few travelers on the new road ever suspected there was a school there except maybe for the flag which billowed in the wind high above the road. After the completion of the new road, it was necessary to create an access road up to the school for buses as well as other traffic to the school.

Ollie Joe introduced me to the teacher as a new pupil in the third grade. I learned the teacher's name was Miss Evans. Thanks to information supplied by Eastern Kentucky University, her name was Laura Kathrine Evans. She welcomed me graciously and assigned me a seat, after I was shown were the boy's cloak room was so I could hang up my winter coat and find a place to put my lunch box. I was accustomed to taking my lunch to school even though Kirksville had a cafeteria, I rarely took advantage of it.

After I was seated I had the opportunity to survey my new environment. The desks were the traditional wood type with a hole in the writing area which was used as an ink well. Most of the desks had been there long enough to have certain graffiti, initials and what not carved into them. If I have my directions right, the front of the building faced north, as Lancaster Pike ran east and west along it's frontage. There was a hallway leading from the classroom to the front door. The hallway was not very long, but quite wide. There were double doors which separated the classroom from the hall. I can recall how Miss Evans gave the student body a demonstration as how not to go through these doors. The doors were solid, no windows, and if someone hit them too fast, someone coming the other direction could get injured.

When sitting inside the classroom, the boy's cloak, or coat room was on the left side of the hall where the girl's was on the right. There was a door which led from the girl's cloak room to a storeroom where school supplies were stored. In the back of the classroom there was an elevated area which required one to go up a couple of steps. This was our library. There were tables and chairs and shelves full of books. There were several old editions of National Geographic magazines which I found to be very interesting. I identified old copies by the advertisements of 1920s' and 1930s' automobiles. On the opposite end, the teacher's desk was located in the center facing the students with a large blackboard on the wall in back of her. To some students it was a treat to be chosen by the teacher to take the erasers outside and pound the chalk dust out of them. On each end of the blackboard, a door opened to two different areas. One door led to a small kitchen, equipped with a kerosene cook stove which was seldom used at this time. The door at the opposite end of the blackboard led to a workshop outfitted with tools, workbench and other implements of useful endeavor. Where Kirksville had radiators in each room providing steam heat, this school was heated by a large heating stove located on one side of the room. It was enclosed by a sheet metal housing with a door leading to the actual stove door. It was fired by coal supplied by Eastern, which the boys were required to carry in to keep the fire going. There was also a large reservoir on top which needed to be filled with water whenever the stove was in use. I personally learned a lesson just how heavy a full pail of water could be, especially when standing on a step stool and lifting it overhead to fill the reservoir without giving myself a bath.

As mentioned, the exterior of the building was brick. There was a portico in the center with concrete steps leading to the front door. There was a rather sizable schoolyard. As memory reflects, there could have been an acre which encompassed the property, even though some may disagree. The land was surrounded by a woven wire fence to discourage adventuresome students with an urge to wander, although this did not happen often. There was a gateway with high wooden gateposts secured at the top with a steel rod leading from the driveway to the front porch via a combination fieldstone and concrete walk. The boys who could jump high enough made a game of jumping and grasping the connecting rod and using it as a chinning bar. There was plenty of room to play outdoor games such as softball, football or other popular amusements. Cracking the whip was a popular game if one could avoid being on the end of the cracked whip. The yard in front of the building and continuing several yards west was reasonably level. However, from the front of the building to the rear and beyond, the terrain sloped significantly. For example, there were perhaps four to five steps leading to the front portico, but there was an extremely high section of steps leading from ground level to the kitchen door in the rear. What we referred to as the basement where the coal was stored, could be entered from ground level in back of the building.

There was a water hydrant located close to the stairs which accessed the kitchen. The water was provided either by the city of Richmond or by Eastern's water system if in fact they had one.

There were separate outdoor restroom facilities for the boys and girls. The relatively small buildings were well constructed having concrete floors. As I recall there was a considerable amount of distance between the two structures. It is not my wish to criticize the school at all for their lack of indoor plumbing during this period. I would be surprised if there was even one student who had indoor plumbing at home at this time. When I started to school at Kirksville in 1940, the outdoor facilities were still being used until the indoor restrooms were completed on the second floor.

As mentioned, there was a flag pole of average height near the yard fence in front of the school building. The boys took turns, Monday through Friday running the flag up the pole each morning and bringing it down each afternoon. We were cautioned, never permit the flag to touch the ground. We felt it would be a cardinal sin if anyone allowed this to happen. We also learned how a flag should be folded for storage. This was during the period when WWII was at its peak, consequently, patriotism was extremely important to each student, be they boy or girl.

After this, in all probability, too lengthy description of the building and grounds, an effort will be made to highlight some of the day to day activities including teachers and students.

I actually began my tenure at the Rural around the first of December of 1943. One could already feel the excitement of the approaching Christmas season in the air. I seemed to have no problem blending into the student body and establishing friendships almost immediately, some, I am pleased to say, have endured until the present time.

One of the sad events early on, was the McElroy family moved away from Lancaster Pike, which meant Ollie Joe would no longer be attending our school. The move must have happened rather suddenly, as Ollie Joe asked me to inform Miss Evans he would no longer be attending. When I gave her the news, it was clear she regretted losing him when she said she was sorry, because he was an excellent student.

I am going to attempt to list the students who attended between December 1943 and October 1947. Please be cognizant of the fact they all were not present at the same time. The scholars appeared to be changing almost constantly. First graders were coming in while eighth graders were graduating. Some families were moving away as others were moving in. It is certain some who were present in this period will be missing from the list since it has been almost sixty five (65) years as of this writing since I first entered the old school. When I first embarked on this venture, I contacted Eastern Kentucky University for help with the names of students as well as teachers. The only name they could supply was one teacher, Laura Kathrine Evans, Miss Evans. The names as best as can be remembered are as follows, not in alphabetical order.

James "Jimmy" Reffet

Joe O'Hearn

Franklin Coleman

Alberta Whitaker

Fred Madden

Shirley Wiseman

Mary Allen Mink

James Edward Hamilton

Lois Smith

Ollie Joe McElroy

Joy Fredricks

Gordon Prather

Mary Coleman

Allen Whitaker

Hugh Madden

Barbara Kay Rowlette

Alan Rogers

Alma Richardson

Jeanine Smith

Wanda Shepard

Eldon White

Charles O'Hearn

Carol Coleman

John M. Winkler Jr.

Rita Madden

Joy Kearns

Frank Rogers

Wanda Cruse

Donald Smith

Donnie Shepard

Buford Blevins

Helen Jane Sharp

Myrtle Coleman

Herman Stocker Jr.

Robert Madden

Denver Madden

Betty Tevis

James "Buddy" Cruse

Chester Richardson

Noland Shepard

Ray Long

Roy Clouse

I apologize if any names are spelled incorrectly as I had no record other than my memory in which to refer.

As was mentioned, the spirit of Christmas was already in the air when I began my academic journey at the new school. Decorations, many of them hand-made, such as chains made from colored construction paper. There was also the very familiar collapsible bells made of red tissue paper. The last school day preceding the holidays was an event we all looked forward to. We knew there was no school work required, but a day of celebration, limited of course. Most schools, especially rural facilities featured a Christmas program and The Rural was no exception. This event was usually scheduled during the daytime hours. Guests were invited, which consisted mostly of the students mothers, as most of the fathers were working. After the program was presented, some type of refreshment was served. Miss Evans made an effort to do this program up right. Somewhere at Eastern, she found a mimeograph machine where she made copies of the program. The paper which the machine dispensed was quite thin. She then found paper more durable in which to tape the printed paper. Each guest was given a copy of the program when they arrived. My mother was given a copy, and much to my surprise, after her death, December 22, 1989, I found the copy in some of her personal mementos. Needless to say, the paper is yellow with age, and the tell-tale blue or purple ink is faded to the point it is hardly readable. However, the program will be duplicated in the following manner.

MUSIC	HALLELUJAH CHORUS FROM THE MESSIAH
TALK	CHARLES O'HEARN
CHRISTMAS BIBLE STORY	JAMES LEE REFFETT
THE OLD WOMAN WHO LIVED IN THE SHOE	HELEN SHARP
RECITATIONS	LOIS SMITH, FRED MADDEN, SHIRLEY WISEMAN, JOE O'HEARN, BARBARA KAY ROWLETTE
SONG	MARY ALLEN MINK
STORY	GORDON PRATHER
SONG	UP ON THE HOUSE TOP

CHORAL READING	REMEMBER
ROPE SKIPPING	
TALK	RITA MADDEN
REFRESHMENTS	
GIFTS	

MERRY CHRISTMAS
and
HAPPY NEW YEAR

Although there was no date on the program, it was December, 1943

It did not take long to establish lasting friendships with many of the pupils, some of which have endured until the present time. Among these were Allen Whitaker, also referred to as "Sonny," and his sister, Alberta, who was known as "Sissy." James Edward "Johnnie" Hamilton. He was already known as Johnnie when I arrived. I never knew why he was called Johnnie, and I probably did not ask. Herman Stocker Jr., whom I always referred to as Junior was a neighbor as well as a schoolmate. I had known Junior briefly when we both attended Kirksville in the early 1940s'. Gordon Prather, undoubtedly the fastest runner in school. There were the Madden children, Robert, Rita, Hugh, Freddie and Denver. Also included are the Coleman sisters, Myrtle, Carol and Mary, who was followed later on by their cousin, Franklin Coleman. I had also become acquainted with Franklin early on at Kirksville. Brother and sister, James "Buddy" and Wanda Cruse. A student who came along a year or two after me was Betty Tevis. Betty's father, Shirley Tevis, operated a grocery store at Caleast, which my parents frequented often.

The foregoing is only a thumbnail sketch of a few people active at the Rural at this time. There were many, many more, as the list of students illustrated earlier in the text shows.

I honestly cannot recall exactly when Miss Evans left us. It could have been before the end of the semester or at the close of the school year. One thing I do remember about her is she was all business where education was concerned. There is one specific matter I have never forgotten about Miss Evans. I have always had a small talent for sketching, drawing and/or painting, art, if you will. Anytime she found me engaged in this activity, she would be critical and caution me not to waste my time on such unimportant pursuits. I will be forced to admit, she was the only teacher in my educational development who discouraged me in this manner. All the others encouraged me. I did not make a point of this in the book, "The Hills That Beckon," but the log house on the cover was painted by the author and the description of the house is found in chapter six, page #21. The original, which was painted in May of 2003 is 16"x 20", is framed, and hanging in my daughter, Melanie's home.

It was clear Miss Evans did not object to all Art forms for which I am grateful. Thankfully, Eastern had provided the school with a portable electric phonograph. Along with the phonograph, several albums of classical music had been supplied. There were RCA "Red Seal" recordings and Columbia "Masterworks," all 78 RPM of course. It was here I was first introduced to timeless masterpieces' such as "Tales From The Vienna Woods" and "The Blue Danube Waltz" by Johann Strauss Jr. and Tchaikovsky's 'Nutcracker Suite." Two of my personal favorites to surface from this classical library was "Hungarian Rhapsody No. 2," by Franz Liszt and "Schubert Serenade" by Franz Schubert. There were also several selections by John Philip Sousa, the march king. It was always fun to observe the kids keeping time with their feet as one of the Sousa marches were being presented. The smaller children were not forgotten as several chorus's were integrated into the program which ran from thirty to forty five minute in length.

It has been said, "music either wears or wears out." I personally became an admirer of classical music as a result of the musical appreciation segment offered by the Rural. I am pleased to say I was not the only student affected by these musical offerings. In a rather recent phone conversation with Allen Whitaker, a classmate I have been fortunate enough to remain in contact. We were discussing the music we were exposed to when he said, "you know, I still like to listen to some of that stuff." I would be willing to bet we are not the only ones.

Miss Evan's replacement was Evelyn Slade. She was somewhat younger and seemed to involve us in extra curriculum activities compared to her predecessor. The Rural student body did not realize it, but we were on the brink of some very exciting days ahead. I am not sure just how much Miss Evans or Miss Slade contributed to what the future held, or if Eastern was the instigator of what was to come.

I doubt very much if any of the rural High Schools in the county at that time boasted an indoor swimming pool to compliment their physical education programs. Much to the boy's surprise, and needless to say, delight, we learned we were allowed to walk to Eastern's athletic building and swim in their regulation size indoor swimming pool. We were permitted this enjoyment once per week for a period of one hour.

In the book, "The Hills That Beckon," in chapter 22, page 99, I describe how I learned to swim in Dry Branch. In August of 2008, I visited the scene of that memorable event. As I traveled down Dry Branch Road and observed what I thought to be the location of this experience, I marveled that I could learn to swim in so little water since there did not seem to be enough to wash one's feet. The point I am attempting to make is the comparison to where I learned to swim and the lavishness to which I was subsequently indulged. The water was crystal clear with depths from three foot at one end to nine foot at the other. There was a diving board at the deep end which saw considerable use. The pool was heated which was appreciated by all, but on occasions, especially in cold weather the temperature level was not up to our liking. Usually before entering the pool, we would test the water with our foot. I recall vividly Gordon Prather checking the temperature and yelling, "it's mellow" and diving in. We had access to the locker room and showers and were encouraged to shower before entering and exiting the pool. We fellows had never been so clean. This opportunity was available throughout the school year. It was probably a ten to fifteen minute walk from the pool to the school, and in cold weather those of us who chose not to wear a hat or cap, would actually find ice crystals in their hair when we reached school. This much appreciated activity was extended to the boys only in the beginning, but later on the girls were permitted to participate.

Evelyn Slade seemed to be somewhat more innovative in her approach to teaching. In the musical appreciation period, she attempted, and was successful to a degree of creating a type of band or orchestra. There was only one type of instrument used. This was a recorder, a wind instrument of the flute family that has finger holes and is blown through a whistle shaped mouthpiece at one end. The manufacturer called this product a "Tone-ette." It was made of a plastic material and purchased in large quantities the price was around .50 cents each. Probably 3/4ths of the pupils purchased one of these instruments. We began with very simple selections, advancing to more challenging works such as Stephen C. Foster compositions. After we had progressed to the point where Miss Slade thought we were ready for public appearance, she set about to find a suitable auditorium for our debut into the world of entertainment, such as it was. She was able to acquire the sanctuary of the First Christian Church in Richmond for our initial presentation. The program was scheduled for 2:00 P. M. on a Saturday afternoon. I had mixed emotions about the time as Saturday afternoon usually found me at the Madison Theater watching my favorite shoot-um- ups. This was a particularly difficult day as I agonized over having to leave in the middle of a Charles Starrett "Durango Kid" flick. I did recover, however, and I guess the program went pretty well.

During this period my family was attending the Peytontown Baptist Church. The pastor, Rev. William R. Royce somehow found out that I played this little instrument and he asked me to play it at church. He could never remember the term, Tone-ette, so he referred to it as a "toe-nail."

In Miss Slade's next project, one must admirer her talent for being able to mobilize a group of boys into doing something they were not comfortable with. As I look back on this activity, it's hard for me to believe any of the boys agreed to participate. She recommended a style show to be conducted at, what was called at that time, "The Eastern Auditorium," now "Hiram Brock." Her idea, devious though it may have been, was to have the boys dress in the latest ladies fashion and parade across the stage while someone supplied the narration extolling the merits of the garments being displayed, accompanied by appropriate music. There were several participants in this unusual exhibit of dubious talent, however, at this time I can recall only three contributors to Miss Slade's ambiguous production. Representing the latest in feminine sportswear was Gordon Prather, dressed in tennis attire with head wrapped in a scarf complete with white shorts, tennis shoes and brandishing a tennis racket. The next victim was symbolizing the modern housewife. The ill-fated individual to fall into this trap was Herman Stocker Jr., wearing an ordinary house dress, head tied with a scarf or bandanna, armed with a straight broom and sweeping as he glided across the stage. Another unfortunate member of the cast of characters was dressed in, of all things, a bridal gown. This person was required to wear make-up and parade across the stage to the plaintive strains of the wedding march. This person will remain nameless, but could very well be the author of this narrative. In fact, he is. Looking back, the whole thing could be categorized as a "drag." Excuse the pun.

Returning to the school, it was mentioned it was equipped with a kitchen with a kerosene cook stove. I cannot remember during the tenure of Miss Evans ever using the kitchen. However, Miss Slade seemed to want to make use of it. Everyone brought their lunch, but to compliment the cold lunches, especially during cold weather, we would prepare something like pinto beans, chili or hot chocolate. The older students would have kitchen detail working in teams of two. Each team would choose what was to be prepared and excused from A. M. classes. One of my memories is working with Robert Madden preparing hot chocolate. We had bowls, cups and utensils in the cabinets, but we had to bring the ingredients from home. The students looked forward to and welcomed these special additions, especially in cold weather. The preparations were fun, not too much can be said for the clean-up.

We were still, for the most part, a small one room country school, even though we were privileged to benefits not available to other educational facilities our size. Where many of the county schools were fortunate enough to have resident physical education personnel, we had none. However, good fortune smiled on us once more in the persons of Paul Love and Betsy Tandy, who were majoring in physical education at Eastern. They were asked, as part of their curriculum to attempt to expand the phys-ed horizons at the Rural in various sporting activities. They were scheduled to appear on a weekly basis of which they could be depended upon to do. Paul Love had an early 1940s Ford coupe with which he pulled a small two wheel trailer with wooden sideboards. He would load we fellows in the trailer from time to time and transport us to the physical education building at Eastern to participate in a variety of pursuits.

At recess, the boys were found to be playing more football than usual and begin to think of themselves as a football power. Paul Love did in fact organize a few games with other grade schools, mainly in Richmond.

When our teacher, Evelyn Slade left us, a replacement was not immediately available. I tried in vain to get information on this woman, for the correct spelling of her name as well as her position, but my communication with Eastern yielded nothing. She was known as Miss Winn or Wynn. I believe her to have been in the English department at the college and was loaned to us on a temporary basis. I have some very pleasant memories surrounding this dear lady. Our midday recess as I recall was from noon until 1:00 P. M. When we begin the afternoon segment of events, she would read to us until 2:00 or 2:30 and no one seemed to mind. Some of the selections she chose were, "Lassie Come Home," "Bambi," "The Boyhood Days Of Abe Lincoln" and "Tarzan Of The Apes." During this early afternoon period there was no problem with anyone paying attention as we were hanging on to each word being read.

Dorothy Moore, a native of Shelbyville Kentucky, was the final teacher during the time I was in attendance at the old school. Everyone considered her to be an older woman, even though she was only twenty four years old at the time. She had a pleasing personality and developed a good rapport with the students.

From time to time we would be treated to a delightful surprise such as being able to attend a movie in the afternoon at the Eastern Auditorium. I can recall one such occurrence when a Laurel & Hardy film was shown. As I recall, the name of the film was "Nothing But Trouble."

As with many schools at year's end a special event was scheduled to celebrate the occasion. I can recall three such activities. In order for these festivities to materialize, transportation had to be arranged. These negotiations usually occurred between the teacher and our customary bus driver. The litigation usually ended with a compromise with the driver agreeing to take us wherever we wished, within reason. One of the conditions, however, was each student was required to provide compensation to the driver for his services.

One of the first such excursions I personally was involved in was a type of picnic at the Barnes Mill area on Silver Creek near the Iron Bridge. There was a rather lengthy grassy area with shade trees between the road and the creek. Our bus driver at this time, as I recall, was William Howard Prewitt. I don't know whose idea it was to choose this location, but as the phrase goes, "a good time was had by all."

A much visited historical landmark in Madison County at that time was the former Merritt Jones Tavern, commonly known as the "Grant House" located at the foot of Big Hill. Legend dictates General U. S. Grant was riding a horse from Tennessee to Lexington when he was overtaken by darkness and spent the night in the tavern. By the time of our visit, the old house had been converted into a type of museum complete with an old gentleman who served as curator. It was rather comical the way he interacted with the kids, especially the boys. He would ask what our Dad's name was, and when told he would reply with something like "yes, I know him." As far as we were from our home range, it was improbable he knew any of our fathers. There was a nice area nearby for our lunch outing, and much energy was expended climbing Big Hill. On the way home on the bus, I'm sure there were some weary explorers. Our bus driver at this time was Mr. Lewis/Louis "Luke" Rogers, the father of Frank and Alan Rogers, who were part of this student body.

The final expedition of this type I was personally involved in was a trip to Frankfort, the capitol of Kentucky. We were all amazed by the sheer size and grandeur of the capitol building with the rotunda, massive columns, and the marble staircases. Our teacher at the time had told us about a room in the capitol building which had a gold ceiling. We were all eager to see this great spectacle, and we were rewarded when we visited The Kentucky Supreme Court chamber. We were also permitted to visit the old capitol which was built in 1830 and had been converted into a museum. There were many important historical artifacts and relics to be seen. This was the most lengthy trip, mile wise, we had taken. I believe the driver at this time was Kay Golden, who had served us for quite some time.

After Eastern State Teachers College became Eastern Kentucky University, the growth was phenomenal. The University grounds along with the many new buildings extended west on Lancaster Pike ultimately swallowing up the old school. In a recent visit to that area, I could not identify exactly where the school was located.

The old school has been gone many years, and now exists only in the minds of those who were fortunate enough to attend.

The Rural Demonstration School

LANCASTER PIKE

At the beginning of the Rural School sketch it was stated the Ted McElroy family lived near where we had moved in late 1943. The McElroy's moved away shortly thereafter. It was also mentioned when the old Lancaster Pike was replaced with the new, great care was taken to reduce the peaks and valleys in the new road wherever possible. The property where The McElroy's lived was owned by Mr. Hugh Million. The property was at the foot of a hill going west, on the right. At one time the house was on the same level as the old road, However, with the construction of the new road, it was built up to the point where concrete steps were installed against a rather high bank in order to access the walk leading to the front of the house. There was a driveway beyond the steps leading to the property.

When the McElroy family moved away in late 1943 or early 44, the John M. Winkler Sr. family moved in. Their small family consisted of Mr. Winkler, his wife, Lelia Newby Winkler and their son, John M. Winkler Jr. There was a married daughter, Nannie Frances Masters. For the length of time the Winkler family lived on Lancaster Pike, "Junior," as he was called by friends and family, and me were buddies and spent a good amount of time together. The Winkler's had a collie type dog they referred to as "Old Ring" who could be hostile toward strangers, but he began to accept me in time. After they moved away, I saw Junior infrequently from that time on. Sad to say, Junior died September 4, 1994 at the age of 58. For some reason, all these years I have remembered his date of birth, June 6th. The Winkler's were good neighbors and could be depended upon in a time of need.

The next family to take possession of this rental property was the Herman Stocker Sr. family. This family consisted of wife Edith*, daughter Dorothy, son Herman Jr. and a younger son, Douglas or "Doug." As John M. Winkler Jr. was called Junior, so it was with Herman Stocker Jr. I had two friends called Junior back to back. It seems the Stocker family lived there for quite some time. As Mr. Winkler engaged in farming, Mr. Stocker worked for a company in Richmond. It was an easy task for me to remember Junior Stocker's birthday as it was the same as my own. We were both born on July 27th. However, I was exactly one year older than Junior. Junior Winkler, Junior Stocker and me all attended the Rural Demonstration School. Doug Stocker did not. He attended one of the Model Elementary schools in Richmond.

Junior Stocker, his brother Doug and me were together almost constantly, especially during the summer months. We explored the hills, valleys and streams in the area, but were always home in time for supper. We had supper back then, dinner was the noon meal. There was one such hill where we could see the white clock tower on the Keen Johnson Student Union building on the Eastern Campus. We swam in the streams and farm ponds and were usually out of sight of adult supervision, which was okay with us. There was a stream, which we referred to as a branch, relatively close to the Stocker residence. For the most part, the branch was the center of our activity. We would follow the branch, in one direction or another in our quest of adventure. I am not sure about the geographical location, but I believe the branch to have been a tributary of Taylor's Fork Creek.

Even surrounded by the beauty and tranquility of the branch and the enchantment of the rolling hills, we still felt the need from time to time to dramatize our day to day activity. Junior and Doug may not remember this event at all, and if they did, they probably would be reluctant to admit it. In the mid-nineteen forties I don't think the term "super hero" had even been coined. We had access to the "cliff hanger" heroes in the movie serials as well as comic books, such as "Spy Smasher." We decided to ask our mothers to produce costumes for each of us complete with mask and cape. No self respecting crime fighter would be seen without a cape. Our mothers did in fact agree to take on this project and outfitted us with the desired apparel.

In order to make this story complete, I must inject another principle character into the drama. The Stocker family, like the Winkler's before them, rented from Mr. Hugh Million. The farm consisted of several acres of which Mr. Million ran several head of horses and cattle. Mr. Million lived just beyond where we lived on Lancaster Pike toward Richmond. He had a bay saddle mare he would ride periodically to inspect the land where the Stocker family lived. He was only interested in the farm to see if the fences were intact etc.

In the words of the late Paul Harvey, "and now, the rest of the story." We three, clad in our new crime fighting togs, feeling very formidable, walked boldly toward whatever danger lurked behind each bush or tree. And you know, there was danger, sort of. After we had gone quite some distance, Junior suddenly stopped and said, "I have a feeling we had better take these things off." Both Doug and me ridiculed him for wanting to spoil our game. Junior was very insistent we remove our garb, hide them, and retrieve them on our way back. Doug and me reluctantly agreed and went sullenly along with him. I will never know what impressed Junior, or what intuition caused him to suggest what he did, but I have always been so thankful for it. We probably had not proceeded another two or three minutes until Hugh Million suddenly rode up. He asked us if we had seen three strange looking people walking the same direction we were going. He said it looked like they had on long coats. (He thought our capes were long coats.) He had been riding on one of the hills and saw us before Junior advised we stash our garments. Of course, we denied seeing such individuals, thus ending the adventures of the terrible trio.

* As this narrative was being written, Mrs. Edith Kanatzar Stocker died at age 102.

As attending the Rural Demonstration School was a rich and rewarding experience, so were the many hours I was privileged to spend with Junior and Doug.

Another friendship developed at the Rural which has endured to the present time is Allen "Sonny" Whitaker. Allen did not live on Lancaster Pike, but Barnes Mill. I would spend the night with the Whitaker family from time to time, but as I recall, Allen never spent the night with me even once. I believe the year was 1944 on a Sunday night, I was a guest of the Whitakers. As I look back now it was unusual for me to be staying with friends on Sunday night since my family as a rule insisted I be in church on each sabbath evening. Also there was the question of school the next day. The Whitaker family consisted of Mr. Allen Whitaker Sr., Mrs. Whitaker, Sonny and his sister, Alberta. Allen was approximately two years my senior while Alberta, whom the family referred to as "Sissy," and me were about the same age. I don't know who came up with the idea, but someone mentioned there was a good movie showing at the Madison Theater. The big budget films were shown at the Madison on Sunday and Monday, sometimes including Tuesday. This particular film was "Meet Me In St. Louis," featuring Judy Garland. My mother had a hard, fast rule. I could attend a movie any day of the week, with the exception of Sunday. Needless to say, I was overjoyed to able to sin in this fashion and I certainly was not going to call to get her permission knowing what the answer would be. The next day when I got home and confessed my sin, she did not like it, but my character had already been damaged and there was nothing she could do about it.

- It was always a pleasant experience to be a guest in the home of the Whitakers. As I recall, it was a rather large two story home. Sonny had a .22 caliber single shot rifle, which I thought was neat. Alberta was beginning piano lessons, and was repeatedly practicing a beginner's piece which I believe was entitled, "wigwam."

When our small family moved from Dry Branch, in the Poosey Ridge area, to Lancaster Pike in late 1943, we experienced a definite change in our life style. We now had the advantage of electricity as well as telephone service.

Our property was located on a paved highway approximately two miles, more or less from Richmond's city limits. Whereas before, we were able to go to town only occasionally, we now could now go at will.

Late 1943 and early 1944 were probably the peak years of WWII. Because of government rationing of domestic steel, and industry focusing on the manufacture of much needed provisions for the military, there had been no domestic automobiles made since late 1941 when a few 1942 models were made. As a result, the used car market was very active. I cannot recall how many different automobiles my father owned during this period. He would drive to work in the A. M., sell his car to someone during the day and walk home in the P. M. It did not matter how old the car was, there was a buyer out there who wanted it. I recall him driving home a 1929 Plymouth. It was equipped with side curtains and had wheels with wooden spokes. He kept this car only a short time. Model "A" Fords were very much in demand, they seemed to run forever.

In chapter twenty one of "The Hills That Beckon," the name, Gene Sebastian was mentioned. I became acquainted with Gene during my many trips to Mike Bogie's store on Paint Lick Creek when I was a resident of Dry Branch. Gene's family lived in the Paint Lick Creek area. Gene was the son of Harry and Beulah Sebastian. Tragically, sometime in the mid nineteen forties, Beulah lost her life as a result of a fire in their home. As one might guess, this unfortunate accident caused an upheaval in the family which led to them moving away from their Paint Lick Creek home. While our family lived on Lancaster Pike, we were next door neighbors to Wylie and Alice Sebastian, Harry's parents. As Harry was attempting to put his life back together after the loss of Beulah, he decided to move in with his parents for a short time. As if he had not been exposed to enough sorrow, his father, Wylie, died soon after he had moved in. I remember when Harry walked the short distance to our house to tell us the sad news. I recall his exact words clearly as my father answered the door. He said, "Jim, Dads gone."

It was during this period Gene and I began to spend a considerable amount of time together. Gene was a few years my senior, however, we were still able to establish a camaraderie due to common interests. I soon learned Gene was very innovative in the creation of instruments which could be used to occupy one's time. With the aid of a saw of some type along with some wooden boards approximately one inch thick, he was was able to fashion something which resembled a hand gun. A clothespin with a spring tension was secured to the back of what was used as the handle with either nails or wood screws. In the days before tubeless tires, inner tubes were available for the asking. Gene cut strips of rubber from the tube approximately 3/4" wide and around 18" long. He then doubled the rubber band, tied it together in the center, leaving a loop on one end and two strips on the other. The idea was to affix the loop around the end of the so-called barrel while the two strips were pulled and stretched to be held securely by the clothes pin. One had to be sure the spring tension in the clothes pin was strong enough to grasp the rubber strips. Armed with these harmless weapons, we could raise our make believe gun battles to another level. When the clothespin was released, the rubber projectile would only travel a distance of ten to twelve feet and would cause absolutely no damage regardless of who or what it hit.

I recall with fondness the time Gene and I were able to spend together, although as I look back, the time was all too brief. Harry and Gene soon found living quarters of their own in Richmond and began to put their lives together. Harry became a member of the Richmond police department where he served several years.

Harry also began to attend the Broadway Baptist Church in Richmond where Rev. W. R. Royce was pastor. Being involved in church was nothing new to Harry as he had been affiliated with an organized body of believers for several years prior to his association with Broadway. On page 113 in "The Hills That Beckon," there is a printed record showing a meeting of The Tates Creek Association Of Baptists which was convened at the Gilead Baptist Church August 23 and 24, 1939 showing church officers. Harry Sebastian was listed as Gilead's Sunday School superintendent. I have personally heard Rev. W. R. Royce make this comment, "Harry Sebastian is the only city policeman who will pray in public." Please keep in mind, that statement was made in the late nineteen forties.

When I no longer saw Gene Sebastian on a regular basis, he was soon replaced by another individual named Gene, whom I would judge was about the same age as the former. Unlike Sebastian, this Gene was a relative. He was Eugene or "Gene" Campbell, the son of

Millard Campbell the brother of my grandmother, Annie Campbell Long. Sometime in the mid nineteen forties, the Millard Campbell family moved to a tenant house on the farm of Brutus Cotton, not a great distance from where we lived. At this particular time the family consisted of Millard, wife, Elizabeth, children, Gene, Wanda, Ronald and Henry. Prior to relocating on Lancaster Pike, the family had lived near the Peytontown area.

While there, Gene had come into the possession of a rather large sorrel gelding whose genealogy traced, without question, to the draft horse breeds. Gene was able to transport, much to his delight, I am sure, this large equine to his new home. Like so many young fellows Gene's age during this period, he had been bitten with the cowboy bug as a result of viewing numerous western flicks at the Madison or State theaters in Richmond. Whatever the former owners of the horse had named him, it did not suit Gene, as he promptly changed his name to "Lightning," something more consistent with a cowboy hero's mount. Gene never endeavored to dress western style himself, even though in his mind he saw his mount exhibiting such distinguishing characteristics. In spite of what he saw in his mind's eye, he never attempted to present Lightning in western regalia. His riding equipment consisted of a plain bridle and a Buena Vista saddle, which was common in that area during this period. No rhinestones, baubles or beads. In fact, at this time western saddles were a rare sight in this community, with the exception for a child's pony. My grandfather, Les Long, had a sorrel mare which he said had Peavine bloodlines. The mare had a foal, a little filly which was also a sorrel. I have been told my grandfather and Gene agreed to trade horses. I know nothing of the details of the trade. One thing I do know, my grandfather never referred to the horse as "Lightning" or used him as a riding horse. He used him as he was intended, a draft horse.

On occasions Gene would join the Stocker brothers and me on some of our outings. He was a good natured individual with a pleasant demeanor and we enjoyed his company.

According to my memory, the family did not reside long in that location before tragedy struck. Millard's wife, Elizabeth was diagnosed with cancer and died while they were living in that small home. As mentioned earlier, Gene was the eldest of the children, followed by Wanda and the two small boys Ronald and Henry. Elizabeth was part of a rather large family with several brothers. After the funeral, Millard and Gene continued to live in that home, however, Wanda and the two boys did not. I assumed they began to live with other family members.

Our family saw a great deal of Millard and Gene until my family moved away in October of Nineteen Forty Seven. Unfortunately for me, from that time I never saw Gene again. I did see Millard on occasions when my family visited my grandmother and her brother happened to be visiting at the same time.

Over the years I have thought of Gene often, remembering the good times we had and wondering what direction his life had taken.

If one were raised in any of the rural areas of Madison County, they, no doubt, were exposed to excellent examples of the equine species. I had always been an admirer of good horseflesh, specially the saddle breeds. For three days in August of 1946, there was an event very much to my liking. Once again, I will refer to my grandmother's scrapbook. She had retained a complete program of this event in her ancient accumulation. I will not attempt to reproduce the entire printed program, but highlights only.

PROGRAM

The Madison County Horse Show

Eastern State Teachers College Stadium
Richmond, Kentucky

Next was a reproduction of a painting of Rex Peavine with the following words.
"The most famous American saddle horse, foaled and kept at stud in good old Madison County."

Thursday and Friday Evenings
Saturday Afternoon and Evening

August 22, 23 and 24, 1946
Judges and announcers were listed next

At the bottom of the first page were these words.
(Exhibitors will please have horses ready for each class at the call
of the bugle)

The next two pages contained the various classes

The back page showed the roster of 119 advertisers, all familiar
Madison County businesses.

Anyone who lived in the mid 1940S' in Madison County and
were at all interested in horses, I feel will have to agree, there was a
Palomino horse craze. It seems everyone wanted a Palomino. This
was no less true at the 1946 Madison County Horse Show. There
were four classes exclusive to Palominos. I still remember that event
clearly and how I thrilled at these fine saddle horses going through
their paces. I can still recall how surprised I was when my father
cheered as a certain five gaited contender made a pass at the rack.

Although the Rural School was not like other county schools
in many respects, the county agent along with his assistants did
attempt to get the students involved in various 4-H activities. Mr. J.
Lester Miller was the county agent at this time. From time to time,
he and a young woman would visit the school and encourage us to
participate in one of their programs. At this time I refer to her as a
young woman, but at that time we probably considered her to be an
older woman since she was in all probability in her mid twenties.
There were certain assistants who were delegated the task of visiting
the students during the summer months to evaluate their progress.
Since my mother always kept Rhode Island Red chickens, I thought it
would be wise, as well as convenient, to choose that project. I might
have watered and fed them a few times that summer.

There was an assistant agent named Mr. Kelly who was assigned
the Lancaster Pike and Poosey Ridge area. Unfortunately, I never
knew his given name. In fact, as I was beginning this writing, I

wrote to the Madison County Extension Office and asked if they had a record of the young woman who accompanied Mr. Miller and also to find Mr. Kelly's given name. However, I have received no reply. Upon Mr. Kelly's first visit to me to inspect my progress with my project, I stood proud and tall as he lavished me with praise in the excellent manner in which I had excelled in raising this flock of chickens. (Little did he know.) He already knew I was a student at the Rural, but somehow in our conversation he learned I was a former resident of Poosey Ridge. It was necessary for him to make calls on a few students from the Rural who lived west on Lancaster Pike, and then various Kirksville School pupils who resided in Kirksville, Round Hill and Poosey Ridge. He was most concerned with locating the people in Poosey since he had no knowledge of that area. He asked me if I would agree to accompany him to Poosey and serve as his guide in finding various folk. When I agreed with his request, he then sought, and received my mother's permission to embark on this adventure. Before we departed I made it clear to him I probably did not know where everyone lived, but could direct him to numerous student's homes. The first 4-H participants we found on Lancaster Pike were Robert and Hugh Madden. We found them clearing a field of some rather large stones. After Mr. Kelly had visited with them for a few minutes, and was satisfied they were meeting the requirements involved, we begin our journey to the mythical land of Poosey Ridge. We did not stop at Kirksville or Round Hill on the way, but planned to catch them on our way back. The first scheduled call on Mr. Kelly's itinerary was to the home of Cecil Francis Prather who lived on Turner's Ridge. Cecil had become a friend when our family moved to Turner's Ridge in 1939. I think Mr. Kelly was a bit surprised, and maybe a little embarrassed when I boldly walked through the front door without knocking, as had always been my custom. As usual, I was greeted warmly by Cecil's mother, Pearl. Unfortunately, Cecil was not at home and I think Mr. Kelly left some literature concerning 4-H activity for Cecil.

Our next stop was to the home of Clay Casey, son of Ollie and Ethel Casey, residents of Dry Branch Road. The Casey's had been our neighbors when when we moved to Dry Branch in late 1942. There was no one home when we arrived, but could hear someone involved in conversation at the top of a very steep hill, directly in back of their home. We climbed the hill to find Ollie, Ethel and Clay working in a rather small tobacco patch. I cannot recall for certain, but this could have been Clay's 4-H project. We retraced our traveled time and distance back to Poosey Ridge Road, turned left and made our way to the home of Garnett and Dorothy Howard, whose two son's Gene (Tarp) and Doug, were involved in 4-H projects. After some searching we found the two boys in the barn where Mr. Kelly was able to share with them what he felt was important to the success of their endeavors.

We might have visited one or two other 4-H achievers in that area, however, the misty mists of time prevent me from getting a clear picture. We made our way back to the village of Round Hill where we stopped at the home of Mr. And Mrs. Elba Tackett and their children. The Tackett family was also our neighbor when our family lived on Dry Branch. By the mid 1940S' it is not clear exactly how many of the Tackett children were involved in 4-H. However, some of them were participants otherwise Mr. Kelly would not have been visiting them. We then traversed approximately one mile south to Kirksville and stopped at Reather Murphy's general store. As with most country stores, even in mid-afternoon, there were several people hanging around. Mr. Kelly asked me if I would like something to drink. When I answered in the affirmative, he treated me to a bottle of 7UP. At this point in my life, I had been a strict cola consumer, Coke, Pepsi or Royal Crown and I did not care for the un-cola, but I tried to force it down. The Murphy's had a daughter, Betty, who was about my age and happened to be in the store at the time. In fact, Betty and me had been classmates when I attended Kirksville School. I believe the Murphy's lived next door to the store. Shortly after our arrival, Betty abruptly left the store. She returned quickly and presented me with a school photograph of herself. It was a rather recent photo as it was dated, 1943-1944. As mentioned, there were several individuals in the store at the time and Betty and me were the victims of a little good natured razzing. Betty may, or may not be pleased to know I still have that photo in my possession.

I made at least one other trip with Mr. Kelly in his search for the elusive 4-H associates. I am not aware of the details which led to his absence, but I saw nothing more of Mr. Kelly. He was replaced by James Thornton, as best as I can recall, that was his name. Mr. Kelly evidently recommended me as a guide to Thornton. I can remember only one sojourn with Mr. Thornton and this was to call on the Lancaster Pike kids. Thus ended my career as a guide to the wilds of Lancaster Pike and Poosey Ridge.

The following is another entry from My Grandmother's scrapbook which was clipped from the Richmond Daily Register in April of 1946. With some help from my cousin, Orline Proctor Hensley, a participant in this event, I was able to establish the year.

The headline reads.
Kirksville 4-H Rally Held Yesterday

The first of ten 4-H community club rallies was held at the Kirksville School, Tuesday, April 16, with Mrs. Helen M. White, assistant state supervisor of Home Demonstration Agents, University of Kentucky, judging the show. Mrs. Wilson Cates and Mrs. Ed Shockley, project leaders, supervised the construction of 72 clothing exhibits. Prof. Carl McCray is community leader of the club. Placings were made by the judge before noon. The style show, held directly after lunch, was attended by teachers, parents and students. Divisions into blue, red and white ribbon groups are as follows:

Towels: Blue, Eva Jean Teater, Barbara Ann Agee, Ruth Rogers and Dorothy Riddell: Red, Billy Jean Baker, Addie Rhodus. Jane Dare Rogers, Emma Mae Creech: White, Orline Proctor, Wanda Napier, Angie Mae Tackett, Ella Mae Ross, Virginia Nolan.

Pot Holders: Blue, Billy Jean Baker, Jane Dare Rogers, Barbara Ann Agee, Emma Mae Creech: Red, Ruth Rogers, Dorothy Riddell, Angie Mae Tackett: White, Orline Proctor, Eva Jean Teater, Wanda Napier, Addie Rhodus, Ella Mae Ross, Virginia Nolan, Virginia Sickels.

Pin Cushions: Blue, Billy Jean Baker, Orline Proctor, Addie Rhodus, Barbara Agee, Ruth Rogers, Emma Mae Creech, Virginia Nolan, Virginia Sickels: Red, Eva Jean Teater, Wanda Napier, Jane Dare Rogers, Dorothy Riddell, Angie Mae Tackett, Ella Mae Ross.

Aprons: Blue, Billy Jean Baker, Emma Mae Creech, Dorothy Riddell, Virgina Sickels: Red, Orline Proctor, Eva Jean Teater, Wanda Napier, Addie Rhodus, Jane Dare Rogers, Ruth Rogers, Angie Mae Tackett Ella Mae Ross: White, Barbara Agee, Virginia Nolan.

Slips: Blue, Wilma Ritchie, Willie B. Jones, Helen Cates: Red, Betty Murphy, Anna L. Rogers: White, Eva Mar Smith, Mollie Napier.

Dresses: Blue, Betty Murphy, Wilma Ritchie, Helen Cates, Willie B. Jones: Red, Eva Mae Smith, Wilma R. Long, Marjory Wilson, Anna L. Rogers and Mollie Napier.

The Peytontown Baptist Church

Members of my family have been members of the Gilead Baptist Church on Poosey Ridge Road for generations. So it followed my earliest memories go back to Gilead. However, since our move from that area, it was determined the distance was too far to attend Gilead on a regular basis. In the book, "The Hills That Beckon," and earlier in this writing as well, there is a reference to Rev. William R. Royce who had been pastor of Gilead in times past. We discovered Royce was instrumental in organizing and was now pastor of the Peytontown Baptist Church, located in the small village of Peytontown. This new fellowship was organized in May, 1944 and since my father and mother considered Royce a personal friend as well as former pastor, we naturally gravitated to Peytontown. We did return to Gilead in the spring of 1944 from time to time but not with any regularity.

This subject has already been referred to numerous times, but I will reiterate. In the early Nineteen Forties my Grandmother, Annie Long begin collecting articles for a scrapbook supplied mainly from the Richmond Daily Register. The Register was kind enough to allow me to include some of these old clippings. Unfortunately, she did not enter the dates when the articles appeared. In the following quote from the Register, It was simple to calculate the approximate date.

The article reads

"The Rev. W. R. Royce, pastor of the Peytontown Baptist Church announces an all day praise and fellowship service

Sunday, June 1st to celebrate the third anniversary of the church. A basket dinner will be served and the pastor is issuing an invitation to all to attend. The Peytontown Baptist Church was organized May 29, 1944 with a membership of 25. The first meetings were held in the old school building. This property has since been purchased and converted into a beautiful church and the membership now exceeds 100."

Ironically, I have in my file an extremely old photo of the student body of this old Peytontown school of which my Grandmother was a member. She was born in 1895 and looked to be six or seven at the time which dates the photo to 1901 or 1902. The photo does not show the school building.

I remember clearly June 1st, 1947, this celebration day. The event was very well attended and as usual there was an abundance of food. There was about a two hour break for lunch and before the afternoon program began at 2:00 P. M. my good friend, Donald Roberts and me tried to figure out how we could skip the afternoon program, as we felt we had already experienced enough preaching for one day. My Dad's car, a 1936 Plymouth coupe was parked at the side of the building facing an open sanctuary window. We thought it would be neat to sit in the car while the services were conducted. We stealthily entered the car, making as little noise as possible and quietly closed the doors. We thought our plan had succeeded until the Reverend Royce, who was standing inside near the window spotted us. He called to us and said, "boys, get in here, get in here before I take a shillelagh to you." Royce was very proud of his Irish heritage and did not mind bantering those Irish terms around. Needless to say, we went inside after our cover was blown.

I believe it was shortly after this event I went forward on a Sunday night and presented myself for baptism and church membership. At this time, baptism's were conducted in a hole of water within a stream called "The Jenny Moss Hole" on the farm of Mr. Charlie Reams. Rita Madden a schoolmate at the Rural Demonstration was also baptized the same day. The Reverend Royce asked me to hold Rita's hand as we waded out into the baptismal waters. At that age I was somewhat reluctant to hold a girl's hand, especially in front of all those people gathered on the bank observing the event. This was in the summer of nineteen forty seven. Neither Rita nor I had any idea which direction our lives were going to take a few short years thereafter. Rita married Claude "C. B." King, whom I am sure she met at Peytontown. Sad to say Rita was taken from us in early 2008.

During the mid- nineteen forties, the Reverend and Mrs. Henry King attended Peytontown along with their twin sons Conrad and Claude. Conrad was known as Connie while Claude was called "C. B". As mentioned, C. B. married Rita Madden. Connie also married a Peytontown girl named Betty Tevis. Both Rita and Betty were schoolmates of mine at the Rural Demonstration School. Betty also lost Connie a few years ago.

Betty shared with me in a recent phone conversation, her father, Shirley Tevis was baptized in "The Jenny Moss Hole."

When our small family began attending Peytontown, there were friendships forged which have endured until the present time.

An attempt will be made to list as many of the faithful Peytontown members as can be remembered in this bygone period. Needless to say, there will be those who will not be included due to the lapse of time. As of this writing, it has been over sixty one (61) years since my family attended Peytontown.

They are as follows, The Ben Roberts family, Roy Smith family, Emmitt Madden family, Robert "Bob" Sharp family, Tevis family, King family, Rose family, Cecil Turpin family, Moss Turpin family, Charles Reams family, J. B. & Minnie White, Middleton family, Russell Rhodus family, Qwen T. Richardson and wife Jenny Mae, John Moody family, James "Jim" Long family and Rev. & Mrs. W. R. Royce.

There were many lasting relationships forged with various families during this period. Among these was the Ben Roberts family. The Roberts son, Donald, and me were about the same age and we became fast friends and spent considerable time together. At that time the Roberts family consisted of Ben, his wife, Susie and their three children, Norma Jean, Donald , Ronald and Ben's father Jacob "Jake" Roberts. A few years later there were two daughters added to the family, Saundra (Sandy) and Patricia (Pat).

The Roberts family were always welcome guests in our home as we were in theirs. During this period, Jello was a popular desert of which Ben referred to as nervous pudding.

Another family we saw often was the Roy Smith family. My mother was very close to Mrs. Smith (Zelma) as she was to Susie Roberts. Mr. Smith (Roy) did not often attend church, so when Zelma wanted to have Rev. and Mrs. Royce for Sunday dinner, Roy would say, O. K., but invite the Long's so Jim can talk to the preacher. The Smith's son, Donald, and me were close to the same age so it followed we saw a lot of each other. There were two boys, Donald and Park, and I believe two girls. One girl was Jackie and I cannot recall the other. A favorite memory for me includes Donald. It was not unusual for a tobacco farmer to allow a son approximately twelve years of age to grow a small crop of his own. So it was with Donald, who was given a small portion of the base to tend. It was his responsibility to take it from beginning to end. I don't know how many dollars were earned, but to Donald it must have seemed like an enormous amount. Shortly after his crop had sold, I ran into him in Richmond on a Saturday afternoon. He was very excited and shared with me his experience as a tobacco farmer. I will never forget the exact words he said to me. "Now you get anything you want, because I have got plenty of money." I really don't think I took advantage of his generosity, maybe a candy bar.

The summer of 1947 saw Peytontown involved in a church-wide bible school. As I recall, this event was very well attended. There was a Mr. Taylor, whom I believe was a missionary home on leave, was the director. He was assisted by Dorothy Sharp, Helen Sharp's older sister. All the Smith children, who lived on a country road some distance from the church would ride one of the work horses to VBS with Donald in charge of the reins. The four equestrians were positioned in the following order. As was mentioned Donald was in charge of the reins followed by Park, Linda and Jackie. Jackie was kind enough to provide the name of the old mare who was called Maude. The horse was hitched to a post which helped support a woven wire fence that partially surrounded the church property. During the breaks, some of the boys, with Donald's permission, would ride the horse around the church property. Sometimes we would get the horse into a canter. During one of these sessions, the Reverend Royce came out of the church and yelled, "boys, don't run that horse, it's too hot." Needless to say, that ended our recreation for that day. Some of Reverend Royce's grandchildren came with him to to these meetings. A grandson, Tommy Royce, a granddaughter, Emma Jo Chambers and another granddaughter whose name, regretfully, I cannot recall.

Looking back now to the mid nineteen forties, the peaceful little village of Peytontown seems idyllic in my memory, and I am sure it was. My life was untroubled like most of my friends at that time. Much of our trouble consisted of how we were to come up with a nickel to buy a coke or candy bar at Moss Turpin's general store which was located, if I have my directions right, the next building east and across the road from the church. As explained earlier, while attending the Rural Demonstration School was a pleasant and unforgettable experience, so was attending the Peytontown Baptist Church.

The Peytontown Baptist Church

Reverend W.R. Royce

RAMBLINGS

The title of this sketch could very well be appropriate for various segments which appear in this document. The American College Dictionary defines rambling, among other definitions, as "wandering about aimlessly and/or "taking an irregular course". In other words, off the cuff comments, one not necessarily related to the other.

The author will take this opportunity to ask a question in this narrative which he has never inquired of his own family members. While the readers may not have any interest at all relative to this subject, the writer apologizes, but forges ahead in his quest for answers.

In growing up in the Poosey Ridge area as an only child, I was very close to my first cousins, The ones nearer to my age were the children of Luther and Mary Laura Long Proctor who were Vernon J. and his sister, Orline. The others were the children of Vernon and Pauline Proctor Long. They were Frances, Betty Jean and Marvin. In the beginning of this writing in describing the John Tudor house with the high door and no steps. It was mentioned my cousins and me would make a game of jumping from the high door into the yard. These were the playmates who participated with me in this activity. Later on, The daughter of Roberta Long and James Agee, Patricia Ann, and Billy, the son of William D. and Ethel Neely Long joined the family. However, by this time we considered Patricia (Trish) and Billy too juvenile to join us in any serious adventures.

Getting back to the original inquiry, which asks the question. Why did I refer to my aunts and uncles by their given names only, while my cousins always prefaced their names with Uncle or Aunt? I don't think it was a lack of respect since I did honor them. It must have been an example set by my father. His father, Leslie Long, was one of eight children, six boys and two girls. The five boys, and one girl, Emma, who was actually younger than my father, was always referred to by their first name by their nephew, Jim Long. The other girl, Jenny Long was married to Robert Oliver. When my father referred to this couple, it was always Uncle Robert and Aunt Jenny Oliver. Why Robert and Jenny were esteemed in this manner I will probably never know, except for what I personally remember about Robert and have learned about him. Robert was a good, no nonsense type of individual. A religious man of excellent reputation and character. I'm sure he earned the respect of Jenny's nephew, Jim Long, while many of Jim's other Uncles such as Sam, Charlie and Marion seemed more like guys he just hung out with. I am reminded there was one more aunt my father referred to as Aunt. She was Nannie, the daughter of Daniel Long by his first wife, Elizabeth Moberly, whom my father saw only occasionally.

I must confess, there was a couple on whom I did bestow this honor. They were the Uncle and Aunt of my mother, Ruby Anglin Long, Noah and Gertrude Anglin, my Great Uncle and Aunt. I always conferred the title of uncle and aunt upon them.

As I am now at the age where I have qualified to order from the senior citizen menu at a restaurant for twenty years, certain questions keep resounding in my memory. Among these are, how many fellows who grew up in the Poosey Ridge area received their first haircut, as well as subsequent trims from Lewis Ward? In the segment "More Country Stores," Neal Burnam Whittaker relates how Lewis Ward sat him on a nail keg and cut his curls which were hanging down while his mother, Mable, sat and cried. This was the store Neal's father purchased from Eb and Sally B. Moberly.

This author is pleased to admit he was the recipient of Lewis's talent when he received his first haircut. I'm sure I was not happy with this harrowing experience which no doubt tested Lewis's patience as well as my father or mother, or both, holding me in the chair until the task was completed.

Lewis would set up shop anywhere it was convenient. On several occasions my Dad and me have gone to Lewis's home to avail ourselves of his considerable hair styling expertise. He would go to anyone else's home if the need arose. Several years ago during a conversation with Cecil Davis, a long time resident of that area, he shared how Lewis would spend the day on Saturday practicing his craft at C. W. Whitaker's store.

I was privileged to renew my relationship with Lewis and his wife, the former Willie Moore Elswick, during the early to mid-nineteen eighties at the Gilead Baptist Church home coming events.

As a child living in the Poosey Ridge area, I learned Fox hunting was a very popular pastime for certain individuals. I am not referring to the type of Fox hunting as riding to the hounds as is practiced in merry old England. This type of hunting in the Poosey area as well as many other regions in Kentucky required much less effort. Unlike their British counterparts who dressed pristinely in their hunting attire, would send their thoroughbreds hurtling over stone fences and hedges in pursuit of the hounds who were in pursuit of, if not the Fox it's self, the elusive scent. The Foxhounds owned by the Poosey Ridge hunters were somewhat different than their English equivalent. While similar to their British cousins, the American Foxhound is taller and more lanky in physical structure.

If there is a difference in the method of hunting on the two continents, the following will show how vastly different the methods are. The Poosey Ridge hunters, consisting of from three to half dozen men, along with their dog or dogs, would find a high hill, build a fire, release the dogs and sit and listen to them locate a scent and begin to follow it. The hunters could usually tell whose hound was in the lead, or whose hound was the first to locate and follow the track. It was mentioned previously how this type of Fox hunting required much less effort than their British counterpart. This type of hunting is a classic example of where the conquest does not have priority, but the chase.

I would never question the motives of these stalwart hunters, however, the little I have learned about the art of this type of Fox hunting is it seems the object of the whole exercise was an excuse to get together with certain buddies, sit around a campfire, talk, joke and occasionally comment on the progress of the dogs. As the fire warmed the exterior of their bodies against the chill of the night, there were those who remembered to bring some liquid refreshment which warmed the interior of the body as well.

After an exhaustive night of this type of hunting which mostly consisted of one trying to convince the other how their dog was superior to the other inferior members of the pack. It was not difficult to identify the baying of such prize hounds as Ole Blue or Yelling Nellie. Even though the object of the chase was never caught, nor did anyone want the pursued creature to fall victim to the pack of hounds which followed. Here again, the thrill of this hunt was in the chase, not in the capture.

One of the prized possessions of some hunters was the Fox horn. Many of the dogs were trained to respond to one or more blasts of the horn, which was usually made of a lengthy steer's horn. There were those who carried them proudly with a rawhide strap or some type of cord. Some more innovative individuals would either paint, or carve designs into their horns. Many of this fraternity became very skilled in the blowing or sounding of this implement. Someone who was adept at using this type of horn could cause the plaintive, if not musical, sound to penetrate the hills and hollows. I can recall as a child attempting to get a sound out of a Fox horn, but was never successful.

At one time this was a much appreciated type of recreation for men in this area. In fact, my Uncle, Vernon Long, was found to be engaged in this activity at one time. At the time this incident occurred, Vernon was living in the Dreyfus (Bearwallow) area and boasted a sizable pack of hounds of his own. He had worked out an agreement with a local country store if and when their supply of meat was kept beyond the date it was to be sold to the public, the storekeeper would save it for Vernon to feed his dogs. When Vernon went to pick up his supply of meat, the owner asked him how many dogs he had, to which Vernon replied, "this morning I counted exactly twenty three."

In amazement the merchant said, "you mean you have twenty three old Foxhounds?", to which Vernon replied, "yes sir, there were three of us boys and I was the only one who ever tried to have anything."

This incident is to be found in Neal Burnam Whittaker's Poosey Trivia. Many years ago there was a featured entertainer, Deford Bailey, on the Grand Ole Opry, who was very skilled on the harmonica. In one of DeFord's musical numbers, he presented the "fox chase," and dedicated it to Bill Long of Duck Branch. Neal says Bill Long was a big Fox hunter.

From what can be determined, this type of Fox hunting has lost some of its luster as the years continue to unfold. I personally new many individuals who participated in this activity, but now I know no one. In a recent conversation with two lifelong residents of Madison County, they each remembered men who were actively involved in this sport, but knew no one today who took part in this exercise. Another question, among many, has this type of Fox hunting disappeared in life's passing parade? It seems it has on Poosey Ridge and the surrounding community. Is it also true for Madison County as well as expanses beyond its borders?

Vernon Long and his Foxhounds

Probably anyone, be they boy or girl, who began their life on a farm in the Poosey area learned early on the importance of

Sorghum Molasses and its role as a food staple. I must admit, I personally never developed a taste for Sorghum whereby I could not appreciate it as many others seemed to. Numerous families would not think of attempting to survive without this very important food supplementary. It seems a twenty five lb. lard can was the proper container to accommodate this prized nectar. However, before the molasses reached the table, or the lard can for that matter, there were certain important steps in its development in order to prepare it for the waiting appreciation of the taste.

The farmers with the inclination to produce Sorghum would naturally be prepared to put in a stand of cane. On page #57 in the book, "The Hills That Beckon," beginning with the last paragraph, there is some space given to the making of Sorghum. I personally have been able to witness first hand the creation of this, so called, "nectar of the gods."

It had been several years, probably sixty five or more, since the author had been exposed to the actual production of this product. The decision was made to do further study in the development of this commodity. The research disclosed Sorghum is to be found throughout the south, but most often in the states of Kentucky and Tennessee.

Companies or individuals who are currently major Sorghum producers, could have mechanized Sorghum mills. However, at the time I witnessed this type of operation on Poosey Ridge, The mills were turned with the aid of a long pole fastened to the harness of a horse or mule which was required to walk in an endless circle. The monotony of walking in a seemingly endless circle was necessary to power the cylinders which squeezed the cane juice from the cane stalks. There were three openings in the mill, one for the cane to go in, one for it to come out, and an opening for the juice of the cane to drain out into a rectangular shaped container in which the juice was cooked. The container, referred to as a Sorghum box was often the same container, or box used in the scalding of hogs at butchering time later in the fall. A steady fire was maintained under the container in order to cook the juice, which also meant the juice was required to be stirred constantly.

In many cases when Sorghum was made, it developed into a community affair, a type of celebration. These occasions were referred to as "stir offs," and were well attended by various ones in the community. As the cane juice was cooked, a white foam begin to develop on top of the liquid. People would get a piece of flat wood and fashion for themselves what was known as a Sorghum paddle. When the small paddle was dipped onto the foam, it hardened almost instantly into a hard candy like substance which was quite delicious.

There was an incident which happened many years ago during a Sorghum making event on the property of my Great Grandfather, Daniel Long, who resided on Moberly Branch. This occurrence could have ended with tragic results, but thankfully it did not. My father, Jim Long, would recount this story from time to time as long as he lived. This occasion involved my aunt, Mary Laura, my father's sister, who at the time was four or five years old, maybe six. Mary Laura was born in April of 1917 which would, at the time of this incident, occurred in the early nineteen twenties. As mentioned, a steady-going fire under the Sorghum box, or container, was necessary to adequately cook the juice. When the juice had been cooked to the desired length of time and the container removed from the bed of coals, a harmless looking white ash was all that could be seen where the fire had been.

If this writer has learned anything in his brief undertaking as an author, it is not to accept hearsay as fact. There is no substitute for going to the original source of the story, if possible. As recounted earlier, my father, Jim Long, who witnessed this incident told his account of the event as long as he lived. I was always told Mary Laura jumped into the innocent looking bed of fleecy white ash, with live coals underneath. From his perspective, it probably looked to him as if she did jump in. However, the subject of the narrative, Mary Laura, tells a different story. At this point in her life, in her early nineties as of this writing, she is physically impaired, but her mind is clear, especially incidents which occurred many years ago. In a phone conversation with her daughter, Orline Hensley, I asked her to get Mary Laura's rendering of her own personal memory of this potentially tragic event. Unlike what I had been told, Mary Laura did not voluntarily jump into the inferno, but as she walked past the site, she lost her balance and fell into the pit of live coals. It seems she did not fall in feet first, but on her knees. I can only imagine the severe pain which raced through her young body as her legs touched the immense heat of the live coals. She said her two brothers, Jim and Vernon, rescued her from this calamity. Her legs, plus other areas of her body were severely burned. She was taken to a local doctor, probably Dr. H. C. Pope in Kirksville since Dr. W. K. Price was serving as county judge at this time.

After a period of convalescence, Mary Laura begin to recover. She said she had to learn to walk all over again. I would be willing to bet when she was exposed to Sorghum making in the future, she gave the innocent looking fire pit with the white ash covering a wide birth.

Les Long and his five children. Roberta seated on ground.
Standing L-R Les, William D. and Mary Laura. Note!
Jim and Vernon peering from behind rosebush.

In the book, "The Hills That Beckon," there was much coverage given to the children of Daniel Long and his second wife, Laura Belle Hickam. However, scant coverage was given to the children of he and his first wife, Elizabeth Moberly. I will be the first to admit the fault is this author's, as his roots trace to Dan's second marriage. Since childhood I have been aware of my Great Grandfather's first marriage, however I was never exposed to that branch of the family. Dan's first wife was the daughter of Charles and Mary Moberly. Daniel and Elizabeth were married November 5, 1878. The rites were solemnized by the Rev. John G. Pond, who beneath his name proudly wrote the word, Baptist. The 1880 census shows Daniel, wife Elizabeth and infant son Thomas living with Charles. The census also states Thomas was born in September of that year. There were two more children born to Dan and Elizabeth, Nannie Belle and Allen B. In the mid nineteen forties, usually on a Saturday afternoon on the streets of Richmond, Kentucky, my father and I would encounter Nannie, periodically, and the two of them would engage in conversation for quite some time. My Dad would refer to her as Aunt Nannie.

Nannie and her husband, Nathan, or Nath Long were the parents of several children. I have personally met two of their children, Daniel and James. A special thanks to Virgie Long, widow of James who was kind enough to provide personal information on this branch of the Long family. The following is an itemization of the children of Nath and Nannie including the year of their births.

Mac, 1905
Gilbert, 1907
Elizabeth, 1911
Daniel Henley, 1915
Betty Ann, 1918
Chester Pope, 1921
Edline, called Edna,1925
James,1930

In recent years it has been my good fortune to become acquainted with Jesse Long of Waynesville, Ohio. Jesse is the grandson of Thomas Burton Long who migrated to Franklin, Ohio around 1910 via a covered wagon pulled by two red mules. He said at one time he knew the names of the mules, but now the names have been lost in memory.

On page #14 of "The Hills That beckon" there is a family photograph of the Daniel Long family which is believed to have been taken in 1910. The large man standing L-R in the back row is Thomas Burton Long. In row one L-R are the children of Thomas and his wife, the former Maggie Lamb. The children are, Jesse Mathew, Betty Ann and Maggie holding infant, Daniel. There was one child yet to be born, Ida Mae.

There is a particular item in the history of this branch of the Long family I'm sure they do not understand. I have thought about it seriously since I discovered the situation, and frankly, I do not understand it either. As mentioned, Daniel and Elizabeth were the parents of three children. Thomas, Nannie and Allen B. I have heard my grandfather, Les Long, refer to Allen as simply, "B." I do not have documentation of their deaths, but Thomas and Allen B. died early on. Allen was not among those present in the family photo which presented Thomas and his family. It is clear Allen was never married, as was Thomas and Nannie. Come to think of it, Nannie did not appear in the photo either.

The particular item referred to above was relative to the last will and testament of Daniel Long. Within the body of the hand written document, there is a directive which will be a direct quote from the will.

> "I devise to Nannie Long and the heirs of Thomas
> Burton Long, two children of mine by my first wife,
> nothing, as I do not desire them to have any part of
> my estate."

The will was dated and witnessed March 29, 1920.

Why Daniel did not wish to include the children of his first marriage in his last will and testament, who knows? There has been much speculation within both branches of the family concerning Daniel's peculiar decision. Dan named his wife, Laura Belle, and two of his sons, Leslie A. and Samuel as co-executors of his will. Laura

Belle did in fact precede Daniel in death. She in February of 1930 and he in late October of the same year.

FINALE

In the book, "The Hills That Beckon," relatively little is said regarding my wife, children and grandchildren. The emphasis was on how things were back then and not the here and now. Within the body of this narrative, there has been mention of my three children, however briefly. I trust the readers will abide the boasting of a seventy five year old husband, father and grandfather. No great grandchildren as of this writing.

My family actually made two attempts to make Columbus, Indiana our home before settling in the second time. We left Lancaster Pike in late October of 1947. When we moved into the city of Columbus, the house setting on a 50' x 150' lot, I felt totally confined, after leaving a home complete with barn on twenty five acres of rolling hills, trees and a stream flowing through it.

Compared to where I had moved from, the land area was like a postage stamp. Needless to say, after a time the hills began to beckon.

My mother was, for the most part, content with the new location since her father, mother, sister and brother also lived near. But, as time marched on, my Dad and I became more and more discontented. In the summer of 1948 we took a week's vacation to visit my Grandparents, Les and Annie Long, who by this time had relocated in the Brassfield/Panola area. The trip back Columbus was a bittersweet experience. Bitter, because we were headed north, away from Madison County. Sweet, because we were planning how and when to return our homeland.

We did return in August of 1948 and for a very short time moved back to Lancaster Pike. I was able to renew my relationship with Junior and Doug Stocker for a brief period of time. I was even permitted to return to the Rural Demonstration School for an even shorter time interval. The very day school started, I was just settling in at the Rural when my parents came to the school to pick me up and announce we were moving to another part of the county. In this locale I was to attend Waco School, which I did from September1948 to March, 1950. While at Waco, I established what I considered to be firm friendships, such as Will Stone and Henry Turpin. I was also re-introduced to two former Kirksville School classmates, Bert Ray Turpin and Curtis Bogie.

In 1948 and 49, the country had not sufficiently recovered from the effects of WWII, and jobs were not readily available. My father was able to secure two construction positions, one from Neville Cotton and later from Burdette Land. By late February or early March of 1950 my father began to doubt if he had made the right decision by quiting his job at Arvin Industries in Columbus and moving back to Madison County. Soon the choice was made. We would be moving back to Columbus, Indiana. I did not like it, but went along with the family decision.

My uncle, Clifford Anglin, my mother's brother was enlisted to drive down in his new 1949 Ford pickup to transport us back to the "Athens Of The Prairie," (Columbus). We moved back into the same house we had vacated in August almost two years earlier. My Dad got his old job back at Arvin Industries and things seemed to fall into place as if we had never left.

In September of 1950 I began my tenure at Columbus High School. There was a group of young people who, in good weather, would walk to the local High School. Among these pursuers of higher learning was a very pretty, friendly, well-dressed and easy to talk to young lady named Sharon Kay Tilley. Cupid was a little slow to act in our case since our courtship did not evolve until June of 1952.

I think it is interesting to share how this relationship was developed. Until 1952 there was no organized body of Southern Baptist believers in Bartholomew County. My parents, who were dyed in the wool Southern Baptists, along with other like minded individuals decided to start a SBC work in the Columbus area. The kick-off event was a tent revival featuring long time Madison County minister, W. R. Royce as evangelist. With much blood, sweat and tears an old upright piano was put into place to assist in the song service. The only problem was, there was no one to play it.

Sharon Kay attended a small church near my family's residence and it was common knowledge she not only played the piano, but the accordion as well. My Aunt, Ruth Anglin placed a phone call to Sharon asking if she would be willing to contribute her talent on behalf of the revival. Sharon did agree to participate and appeared that first evening, much to my surprise, as well as delight. She also agreed to lend her expertise to subsequent meetings.

For the premiere of Southern Baptist activity in this area, W. R. Royce, long time Madison County minister was called to conduct the initial series of meetings

Sharon and I begin to see quite a bit of each other after the chance meeting at the newly established church, and to use a well worn phrase, "the rest is history."

We were married October 29, 1954, and as of this writing have celebrated fifty five years of wedded bliss.

For the record, the following will be a brief representation of our children, their spouses and grandchildren. As of this writing there are no great grandchildren.

Our first was our daughter, Kathy Rae, born November 19, 1955. Kathy attended elementary and high school locally, and also attended Indiana University for two years until she and Merrill Jerome "Jerry" Moore were married in August of 1976. Jerry, also a student of I. U. graduated that same year. They have one son, Matthew.

The second was our son Timothy J., born August 7, 1959. Tim, like Kathy, attended school in the local Columbus school system. Tim, his wife Margaret (Maggie) and the children, who still live at home, reside in Louisville, Kentucky. The children are James Leslie Long, named for his Great Grandfather whom we call Jimmy lives in Tucson, Arizona. Andrea René, a resident of Bloomington, Indiana. Amelia Stephanie, of Louisville and a step daughter, Aurora Murrell, also of Louisville.

The third child to round out our family circle was Melanie Anne, born July 28, 1966. Melanie sought her education at various schools of learning beginning with Vincennes University, Indiana University and the New York State College of Westbury. In the late Nineteen Eighties, Melanie was a resident of Long Island, New York. An interesting development occurred when Melanie returned from New York and began work locally in an Outlet Mall for a clothing store. A young man came into the store looking for some shirts. She noticed he had a distinct New York accent. Further conversation revealed he lived near where she did on Long Island, however they had never met. After this historic meeting the two began to see each other on a regular basis.

Melanie and Eric John Knechtel were married in December of 1993. They are the parents of three children. They are, in chronological order, Ashlyn Kay, Spencer James and Nicole Elizabeth.

To say I am proud of my children and grandchildren as well as the spouses of the three is not reinforced to adequately convey my feeble attempt to express my true feeling. There are those grandchildren I do not see as often as I would like, however, I am privileged to have four who live in the same community whom I see regularly.

Jerry Moore was the only spouse of my three children my father was privileged to know. I have heard him say, from time to time, he appreciated Jerry. I too must say I appreciate him more and more as the years unfold.

It did not take long for Eric Knechtel to win the hearts of the new family he joined after his marriage to Melanie. This Long Island New York transplant adapted well to the sometimes dubious Hoosier culture. He and Jerry have been very important additions to our family.

There is one daughter-in-law, Margaret Sherman Long, whom we refer to as "Maggie." When I was struggling with the writing of "The Hills That Beckon," she helped me in a wonderful way by typing manuscripts and later adding what had been written to a computer floppy disc. When I started the process, I did not have a computer, therefore, she gave me much valuable guidance and direction. Thanks, Maggie, both Sharon and I are pleased to have you as part of our family.

The author and editor, Ray and Sharon Long

Jerry, Kathy and Matthew Moore

The Tim Long Family Row One L-R Jimmy, Andrea and
Amelia Row Two L-R Maggie, Tim and Aurora

The Eric Knechtel Family Row One, Nicole Row
Two Melanie, Ashlyn, Spencer and Eric.

This publication is my third attempt as a would be author, and as always, I struggled with how to begin and also, how to bring it to a close.

In the forward, the statement was made as to how many folk were gone before the publication of "The Hills That Beckon," who willingly contributed to its content. At this point and time it would be difficult to name all of these willing participants. Even though some contributions were small, each was so appreciated. Even a small addition is certainly not insignificant.

When at last I had seized upon the idea a sequel would be attempted, certain details began to pervade my thoughts, such as, how many stories are there which have not been told? How many families deserve to be mentioned who were not? Needless to say, it would be virtually impossible to tell all the stories which abound, or comment on all the Poosey Ridge families who were not included. However, it was a distinct honor to be able to feature certain families and individuals who were not referenced in the original publication.

The most rewarding testimonials this author was privileged to receive came from readers who concurred reading "The Hills That Beckon," was similar to reading their own life story. It seems to mean a great deal to certain people when they can see their name or a family member's name in print. It has been my intent to include as many names as possible in the writing of these two books.

I suppose one could say, the purpose of these two narratives was to stimulate the memory of the reader. If the reader happen to be of a certain age, he or she could identify with the topic in question. If a younger person, they no doubt have heard the subject matter, be it individual or tall tale, told by relatives or friends.

The goal of the author in the publication of these two memory collections was in some small way bring a little happiness to the reader by reminding them of people, places and events which were familiar to them.

If by what is written, a pleasant memory is rekindled which brings a smile or a sense of well being to the reader, then the author's goal has been accomplished.